THE NEW ENGLAND LIFE OF CARTOONIST BOB MONTANA

Beyond the Archie Comic Strip

• CAROL LEE ANDERSON •

THE History PRESS

Published by The History Press
Charleston, SC 29403
www.historypress.net

First published 2013

Manufactured in the United States

ISBN 978.1.60949.786.6

Library of Congress CIP data applied for.

This book is dedicated to my son, Dean, who is not only a cartoonist in the making but also the best son a mother could have.

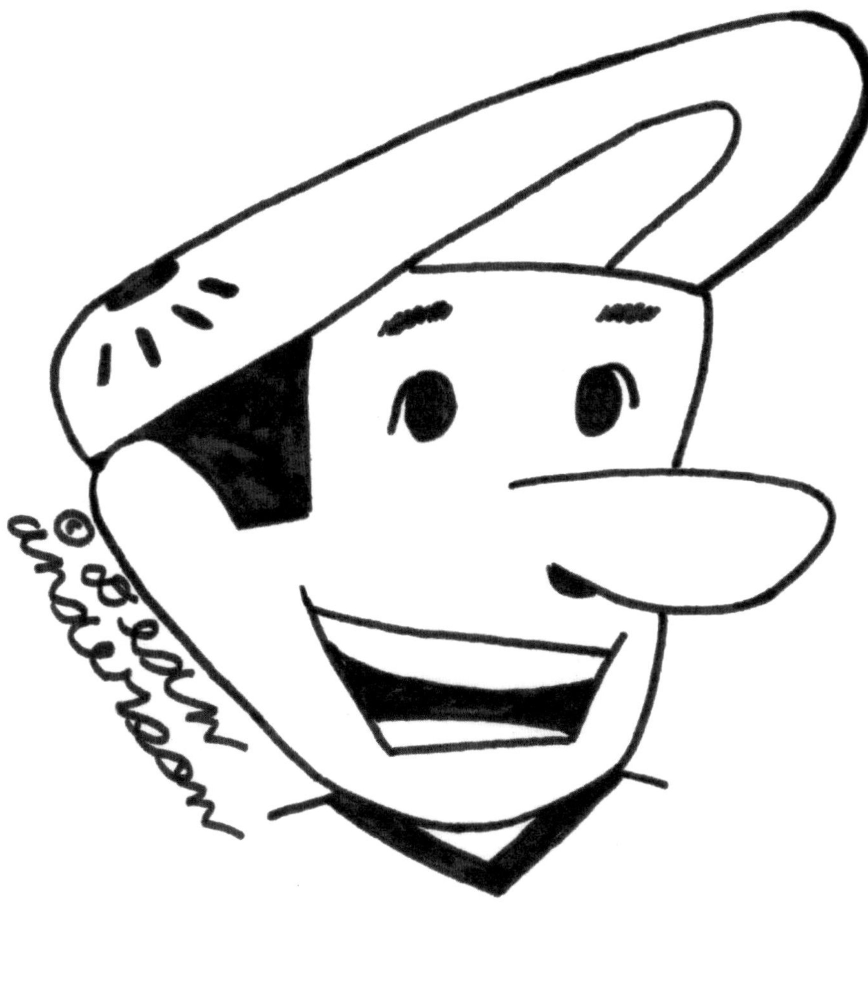

contents

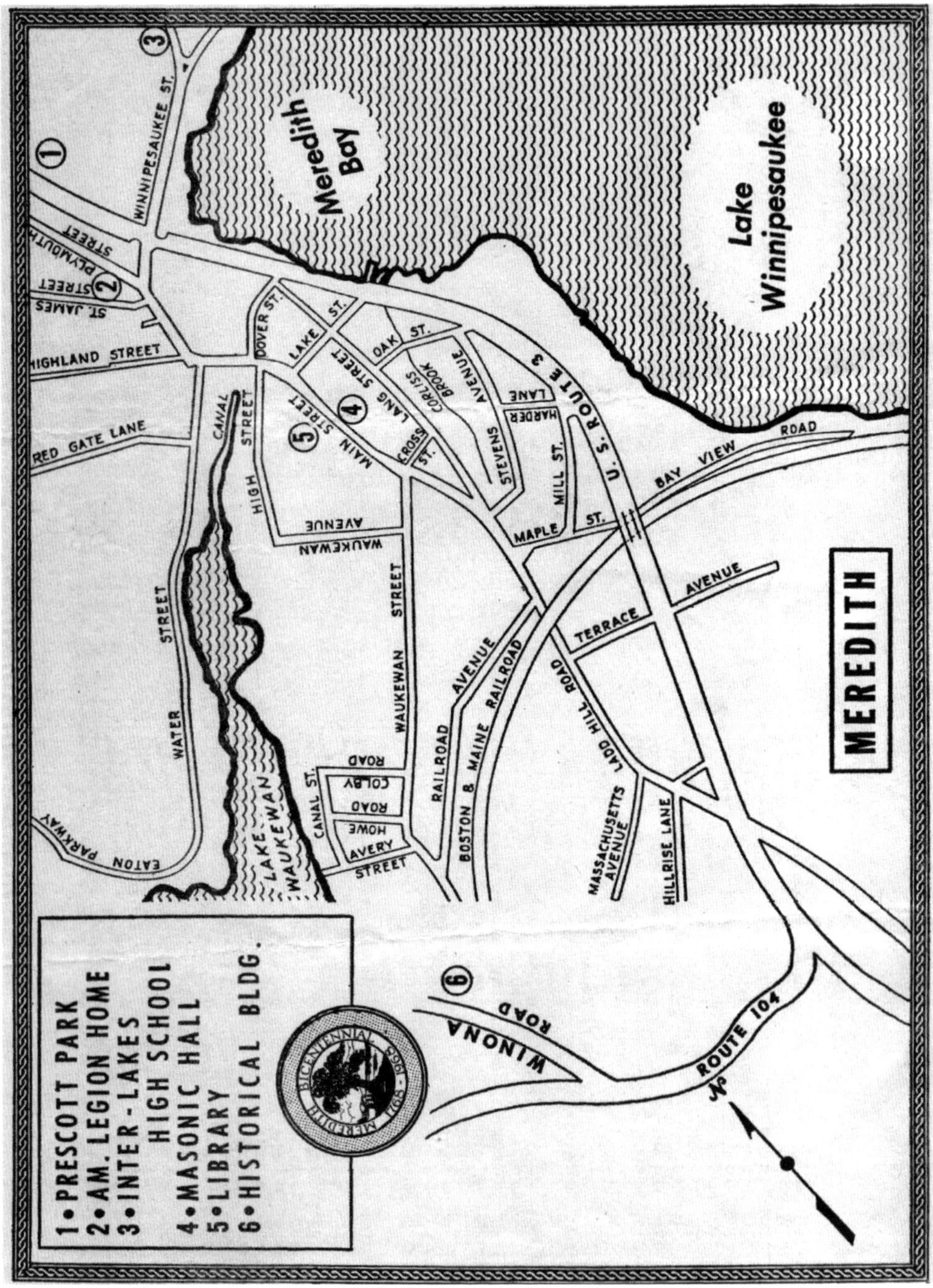

Map of the town of Meredith, 1968. *Courtesy of Meredith Historical Society.*

Foreword

Bob Montana—a friend and a neighbor. We settled, lived and celebrated life in Meredith, New Hampshire. We had similar dreams, desires and goals, and we orchestrated our desires to entertain. Bob gave us his creativity. There are few men who could embrace life with such humor.

Bob's conviction to achieve and make a difference through his creative accomplishments was a focus in his giving. He inspired many to perform their art regardless of its media. He gave me the inspiration to share my talents through music, theater and writing. He embraced his creativity with humor—a romance via his life. He showed this love through his family, community and friends.

Bob saw humor in natural occurrences in school with his characters Archie, Veronica, Betty and Jughead. What we feel is natural, and he made it his humor.

Professionally, to remember Bob's affection of the school programs would be through his artistic contribution. For hours, he would masterfully design stage sets and program covers. His participation in fundraising projects and theater presentations made the activity enjoyable by his unselfish artistic donations.

The Montana family embraced their school and community through the arts and their lives. A highlight came from his boys, who created a thirty-two-foot mural celebrating the music of the Beatles that was displayed in the music room for many years.

Bob was highly respected by his peers. My fond memories of the Montanas cannot be expressed by words alone. However, Carol Anderson has captured the essence of Bob Montana's life through his celebration of family and friends. To read his biography is to be inspired and embraced by his love for life. This book is a must!

BRUCE HEALD, PHD
Adjunct Professor of History
Plymouth State University

Acknowledgements

I will be forever grateful for the opportunity to write a book about the New England life of cartoonist Bob Montana. During the course of researching and writing this book, I gained many new insights into life. More importantly, it gave me a friendship with Bob Montana's daughter, Lynn Montana, which has been a blessing not only to me but to my family as well. Lynn is the perfect blend of her mother's elegance and her father's wit and creativity. Without her friendship, conversations, generosity and encouragement, I could not have written a book that would be anywhere near a fitting tribute to her father. I am deeply thankful to her for never wavering from the belief that I could overcome the intimidation I felt about putting the story of her father's life into words. I also wish to thank Bob's children—Lynn, Paige, Ray and Don—for granting me permission to use some of their amazing family photos within the pages of this book.

I first met Dr. Bruce Heald when we were both signing our respective books during an author event. Little did I know at the time how connected he was to Bob Montana. As I researched Bob's life, I smiled when I learned that the two men not only knew each other but were also close friends. I am honored to have his foreword grace this book, and I am equally honored to call Bruce my friend.

Paul Miller, along with Bob Montana and other artists, created an artist's colony in Meredith that could never be duplicated. The talent of these artists knew no boundaries, and they were steadfast friends. I fully appreciate and will never forget Paul's willingness to share some of his thoughtful memories despite having to deal with an extremely busy schedule. His thoughts and recollections filled in many of the gaps in my research, which would have remained were it not for him.

Steve Hulse could not have been more articulate when I asked him to put his favorite memories of his friend Bob Montana down on paper. He took the time to think through what he wanted to share, and his words will give the readers of this book some wonderful insights into how the cartoonist viewed the world. I wholeheartedly thank Steve for telling me in each and every one of his emails that he had no doubts that I could write a great book about Bob, his life and his contributions.

When I asked Marie Jose Malarge to write about the time she spent living with the Montana family, she graciously offered many of her heartwarming memories on several occasions. I thank her for her candidness and lovely words, all of which she has allowed me to place within the following chapters.

Bill Allen and his wife, Lynn, were such delightful hosts when I interviewed them at their home. We discussed Bob Montana, the Allen Barber Shop, life in general and all things in between. Their thoughts and memories kept me inspired and, at the same time, provided me with critical information. Bill is a dedicated historian just as his father was before him, and I sincerely thank both Bill and Lynn for their stories of Bob Montana and growing up in Meredith.

I thank Meredith Library Director Erin Apostolos and her friendly staff, especially Christopher Leland, for the patience and assistance they offered when I was conducting research at their library. After having spent months there poring over past editions of the *Meredith News*, I wasn't surprised when Erin said that she was beginning to consider my son and me part of the library's staff. We completely enjoyed the time we spent there, quietly giggling over *Archie* comic strips and just being part of life in Meredith.

Thank you to everyone at the Meredith Historical Society—especially President George Jewell—for allowing me to scan their collection of pertinent images and also for granting me permission to use them. Their work to preserve Meredith's history is impressive and provides a vital service to both the town and historians alike.

Bob Lawton, founder/publisher of the *Weirs Times* and owner of Funspot, the world's largest arcade, is one of the most inspirational men I have ever met. His abundance of energy, optimistic outlook and impressive contributions to the community are second to none. I knew that each time I called him with a request, his answer would always be, "Anything you need!" I thank Funspot's webmaster, John McGray, for quickly supplying me with a copy of the Funspot jester logo.

Doug Leich, scholar and author, tragically passed away just a few months after we met. He wanted so much to pass along to me the tremendous amount of information he had gathered for his book, *Passion for Skiing*. Thankfully, his wife, Holly Vanostrand, continued to assist me after Doug's death, providing me with valuable information about the Dartmouth Winter Carnival, of which Bob Montana was a huge fan.

I so appreciate the endless hard work of everyone at The History Press. The publication of this book would never have happened without the dedication of Commissioning Editor Jeff Saraceno. He never failed to cheerfully help me find my way through the sometimes-overwhelming stages of writing a book. Thank you also to Commissioning Editor Mattie Sowash and Project Editor Will Collicott for the editing of this book and for dotting each "i" and crossing every "t" when I didn't.

Harrison Haas, one of my dearest friends, is a rising star in the field of photography. I can't thank him enough for always being so willing to jump into a project and capture spectacular images when I ask for them. His easygoing personality makes him a joy to work with; his patience and creativity will never cease to amaze me. There is no doubt that the talent and dedication he possesses will take him incredibly far in life.

I am eternally grateful to my husband, John, for standing beside me through thick and thin and for being my biggest fan. I couldn't accomplish half of what I do without his constant encouragement and the support he offers in so many ways. Somehow, he manages to keep up with my fast-paced life with a style all of his own—and always with a smile.

I thank my children, Sarah and Dean, for giving me the perspective that anything is possible in a world filled with obstacles. They have taught me far more than I could ever teach them. Watching them grow up has been the biggest thrill of my life, and everything I do, I do for them.

Introduction

The mere mention of the name "Archie" will, for many adult Americans, bring back memories of simpler times, when faithfully reading *Archie* comic books was an adolescent ritual. That clean-cut teenage boy with the toothy grin and saddle shoes burst onto the American scene in the early 1940s and fortunately never left. His troubles, frustrations and problems are common to the world's teenagers, giving them the belief that if their pal Archie and his friends could survive the turbulent years of high school, then so could they.

Cartoonist Bob Montana drew the first *Archie* comic book in Meredith, New Hampshire, while renting a cottage on Lake Waukewan in 1942. It became a smashing success, immediately becoming one of the most popular comics in American history, a popularity that remains strong even today. Later, in order to offer eager fans even more adventures of their favorite teenager, he created the *Archie* comic strip in 1946. It would go on to appear in hundreds of newspapers across the country and throughout the world.

It was Bob who breathed life into each one of the characters in *Archie*, giving them all unique personalities, complete with their own lovable quirks. Their mistakes are not unlike our own, and their ability to find innocent humor in life's mishaps is a gift from the cartoonist. He taught us not to take life—or ourselves—too seriously.

Much has been written about *Archie*, far less about Bob Montana and too little about his life in Meredith, the town where he lived, worked and raised his family. A quiet and shy man by nature, he did not seek out opportunities for interviews and never thought of himself as a celebrity. He was simply a cartoonist that strived to be the best.

When Bob wasn't at the drawing board, he was fully involved in town activities that often included directing amateur plays, fundraising for local charities or supporting youth organizations. The lack of information about his life beyond *Archie* has left a void in documented history on many levels. His numerous, long-lasting contributions to his community are often overlooked, leaving half the story of his impressive life untold.

"Good, clean fun" is how Lynn Montana described the humor in her father's comic strip on the day I first met with her to discuss my idea of writing this book. We had agreed to meet for coffee at Kara's Café and Cakery in Meredith, and the weather couldn't have been more perfect. It was bright and sunny, with just enough of a breeze to blow the napkins off our table. We chose to sit on the porch and look out upon Main Street, where traffic still moves slowly. Typical of many small New England roads, it was designed during an era of far less people and even fewer cars.

As Lynn talked about her father and their family life in Meredith, I began to fully realize that what I saw around me was indeed the town Bob Montana loved and the place he called home. Many of the buildings that stood when he was a resident still remain, including his former art gallery just a few doors down from where we were sitting. The Allen Barber Shop, the Yarnery and Grad's, all establishments that were featured in the *Archie* comic strip, have long disappeared from Main Street. The historic buildings that once housed long-standing enterprises frequented by loyal customers now hang the signs of modern businesses above their entrances. Meredith has changed to keep pace with the times, but the lovely New England town that Bob drew into *Archie* is still visible.

There was a certain magic to Lynn's stories, especially since I had recently discovered that her father often included local scenes and people in his strip. When I was conducting research for my first book, *The History of Gunstock: Skiing in the Belknap Mountains*, I was surprised to find that Gunstock, a New Hampshire ski and recreation area, had been the focus of an *Archie* comic strip in 1947. My goal after finishing the book was to find out how many times Bob had included someone or something from the area.

It didn't take long for me to see that the comic strip was packed with local scenes, personalities and events. My desire then became to write a book about Archie's connection to New Hampshire and then also detail some of Bob's life in Meredith. After receiving Lynn's blessing to write this book during our initial meeting, I set off, determined to learn every fact about Bob Montana.

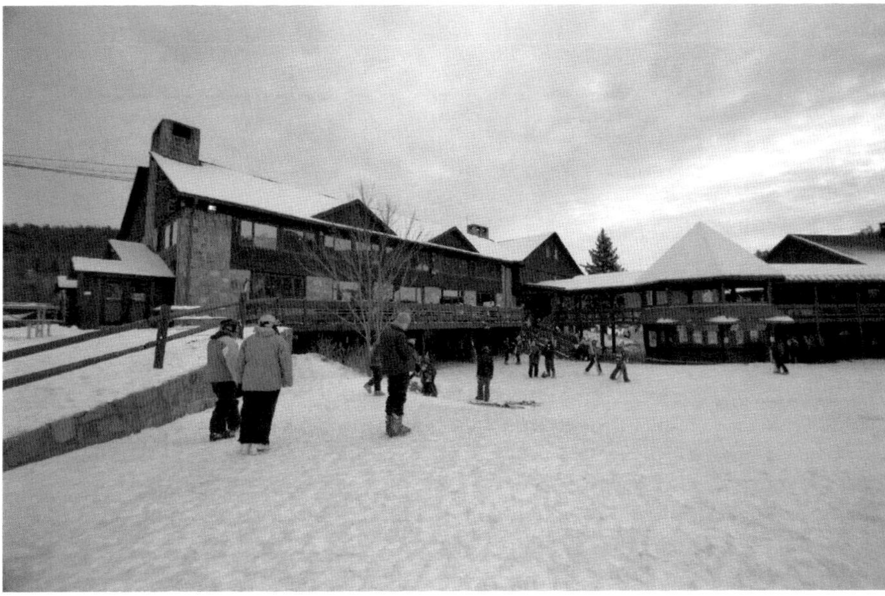

The historic main lodge at today's Gunstock Mountain Resort, formerly called the Belknap Mountains Recreation Area. *Photo by Harrison Haas.*

My son and I spent several mornings a week for months at the Meredith Public Library, a place that Bob had continually supported in every way possible. The list of locals in the strip grew to be extensive, as did the list of articles about the cartoonist and his family. Bob was a tremendous role model, and a book about his life couldn't be written without including the positive influence he had on those around him.

It became obvious that *Archie* was far more than just a brilliant comic strip. Just as Bob had kept an illustrated diary while a student in high school, the comic strip became his adult diary. The adventures of Archie and his pals mirrored Bob's adventures in New Hampshire. Whether he meant to be or not, the cartoonist was also one of the best historians in the area. By drawing local individuals and events into *Archie* for nearly thirty years, he had carefully chronicled the historical events and characters in the Lakes Region.

Writing a book about such an extraordinarily gifted man was daunting to say the least. However, it was Bob who wrote his life story by the way he lived and the contributions he chose to make. My job was to transfer that into words. This book honors one of America's most comical, talented and generous men. It is the story of Bob Montana's life in New England and the legacy he created—beyond the *Archie* comic strip.

Chapter 1

Montana the Cowboy Banjoist

He walks out upon the stage in pure white buckskin, silk, broadcloth and silver trappings.
—Metronome, *1926*

To fully comprehend the genius, personality and extraordinary talents of cartoonist Bob Montana, it is essential to examine the depth of brilliance that existed within his family. An overabundance of creativity and independence went hand in hand with the Montana name. In addition to possessing a natural artistic talent, it was Bob's childhood experiences that molded his sense of humor. Those unique circumstances sharpened his ability to keenly observe and later record the humorous side of human behavior.

Bob's father, Raymond William Coleman, was born on July 31, 1880, in Emporium, Pennsylvania. By the time the young lad turned ten, his family had moved east and settled on a farm in New Hampshire. Raymond showed an intense interest and talent for music early in life, and as fate would prescribe, the young would-be musician was given a banjo by a friend of the family. That gift started a life-long love affair with the instrument and the romance of music. Later in life, he reflected on the adventure of receiving his first banjo in an article he wrote for *Metronome* in 1926:

> *As Grimes would say, a long time ago, one sunny day a carriage load of friends drove up to our front gate of the farm where I lived near Rochester, NH. Among them was a gentleman (I say gentleman because at that time*

I did not know he played a banjo), who was an attorney and who had learned to play the banjo while at college. He had an old banjo at home that he did not use anymore…and if I could learn to play a tune on it before he came up again, he would give it to me.

At last the banjo came, an old Stewart—no head, no keys, no strings, just the rim and a neck on it. Brass top hoop and brackets tarnished black. However, I went to work on the task of making something out of it and then learning to play something on it. I whittled keys out of hickory. I carved out a tailpiece and a bridge. The drummer in the town band gave me a broken drumhead which was large enough to make a head for the banjo. I soaked the head and put it on the banjo and of money I had saved by trap shooting received a set of new banjo strings from Rochester. This completed the reconstruction, and the next thing was to learn how to tune it.

About fifteen miles from our farm lived an old maid who, it was said, played a banjo. I wrote her, and in a week or so, I had an answer stating that she could give me lessons for fifty cents each. So, one day, I started for her home on our best horse with the banjo in an old wheat sack. I arrived there about noon, and they were very kind to me. They put the horse in the barn and fed him and took me right into the house for dinner. After dinner, we got out the banjo, and I received the first and only lesson I ever had.

In this lesson, I learned to tune the instrument and played one chord, the first chord in C. I guess the lesson lasted about two hours, and then after the teacher had played all she knew for me, I started for home after paying her the fifty cents for the lesson, the dinner and having the horse taken care of. When I had covered about half the distance to my home, it became dark, and the moon came out. And as I rode along thinking of the banjo, I began to worry about the system for tuning and thought I had forgotten how to tune the banjo.

I had the system for tuning written on a little slip of paper, and so I dismounted, tied the horse to the fence and sat there in the moonlight on the fence and practiced for an hour. From the way that horse pricked up his ears and looked at me, he must have thought I was plum crazy. Maybe I was, but I just kept on getting more crazy over the banjo, and before long, I was playing with an old-time fiddler for country dances, and that was the beginning of my greatest venture.[1]

That was indeed the beginning of something great; music had taken a firm hold of him—it became his life's passion and gnawed at him when he wasn't performing. As he grew up on the family farm, he played the banjo during idle moments and worked incessantly to improve his musical techniques. During the summer season of his last two years of high school, he labored as a cowboy on his uncle's ranch not far from Fort Benton, Montana. It was there that he perfected what would become his well-known plectrum style of playing, with which he could make one banjo sound like two. While relaxing around the campfire after a full day's work, Raymond and a fellow cowboy would play banjo together for hours. Those two seasons spent in Montana had a profound effect on him and would forever guide the direction of his life.

By the time his days in school drew to a close, he was almost eighteen, and the Spanish-American War had become his focus. He quickly volunteered to become a soldier, and by June 1898, he had reached Cuba and was ready to fight. Combat was not in the cards for this soldier. Instead, a fall off of a transport wagon caused him to break both arms, and he returned home after never firing a shot.

Nearly a year later, during the spring, Raymond was anxious to travel and perform, so he joined the C.S. Shaw Overland Circus for one season. Showing the ease with which he could play different instruments, he played the trombone for the circus and saved his expertise on the banjo for the variety concert held after the show.

Once the season was finished, Raymond made an earnest attempt to study law at Cornell University that fall. He remained there as a serious student for two long years. With constant thoughts of taking his banjo show on the road, the bright young man found it difficult to concentrate on his studies. Being true to himself and his talents, he chose to forego the almost-guaranteed financial stability of a lawyer's life in favor of becoming a musician and a performer. His promising career as a lawyer ended; he left school, never to return.

No longer feeling like his wings were clipped, Raymond immediately joined the Willy West Minstrels and then moved to the vaudeville circuits, Keith and Pantages. Combining his love for the state of Montana and for his passion for the banjo, he called himself Montana the Cowboy Banjoist. There was nothing that could stop this young musician from pursuing his dream, and it was clear that he had made the right choice. Not only was his career as a banjoist skyrocketing, but he also met the love of his life while on tour. A beautiful dark-haired, dark-eyed dancer in the Ziegfeld road show of the *HMS Pinafore* caught his eye—and his fancy. The lovely young lady was Roberta Georgina Pandolfini, but while touring, she was known as Bobby Gerald. Roberta was undeniably regal. Her grace and elegance easily gave away her secret that she was of a noble Italian bloodline; her grandmother was Countess Pandolfini of Florence.

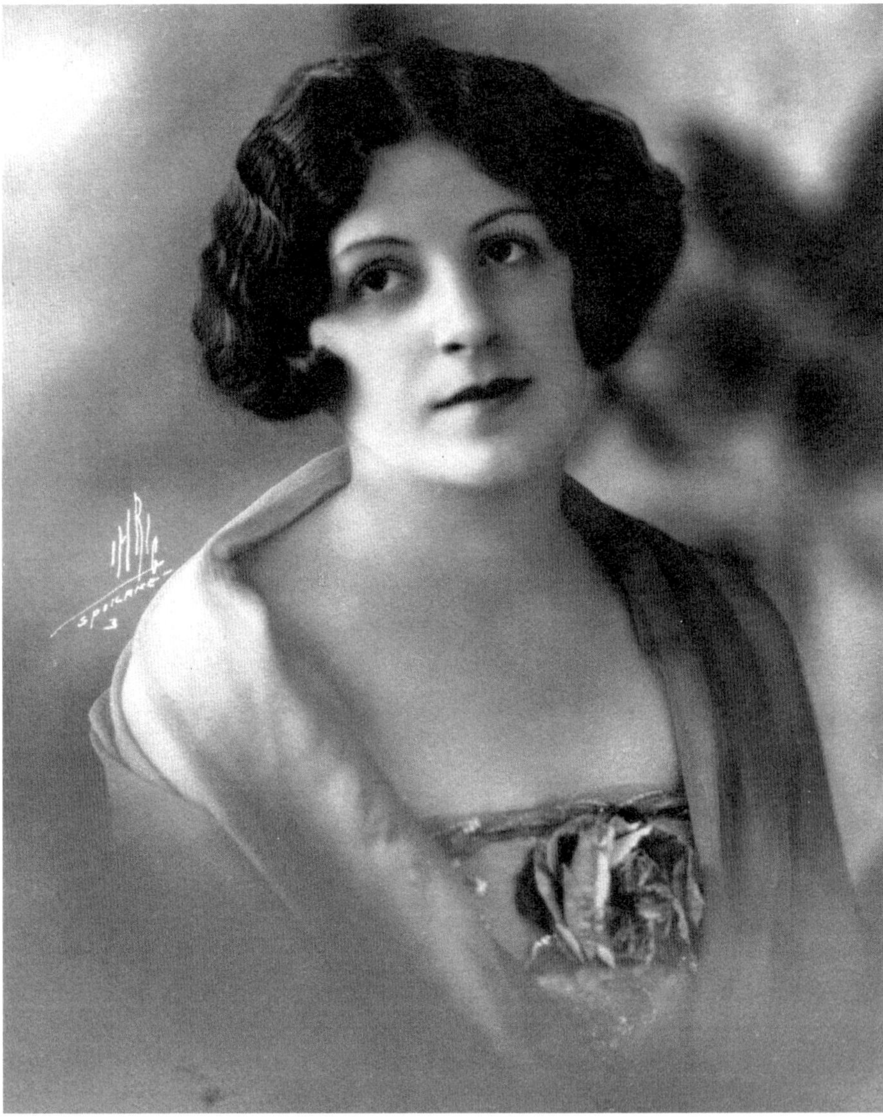

Roberta Montana, mother of Bob Montana. © *Montana family*.

Raymond and Roberta were married on October 21, 1916, in New York, where they lived when not on the road. One year later—almost to the day—their first child, Ruth, was born on October 22, 1917. The threesome stayed in New York, but as the 1919–20 touring season approached, Raymond decided to again join the circuit. As was the custom for young children

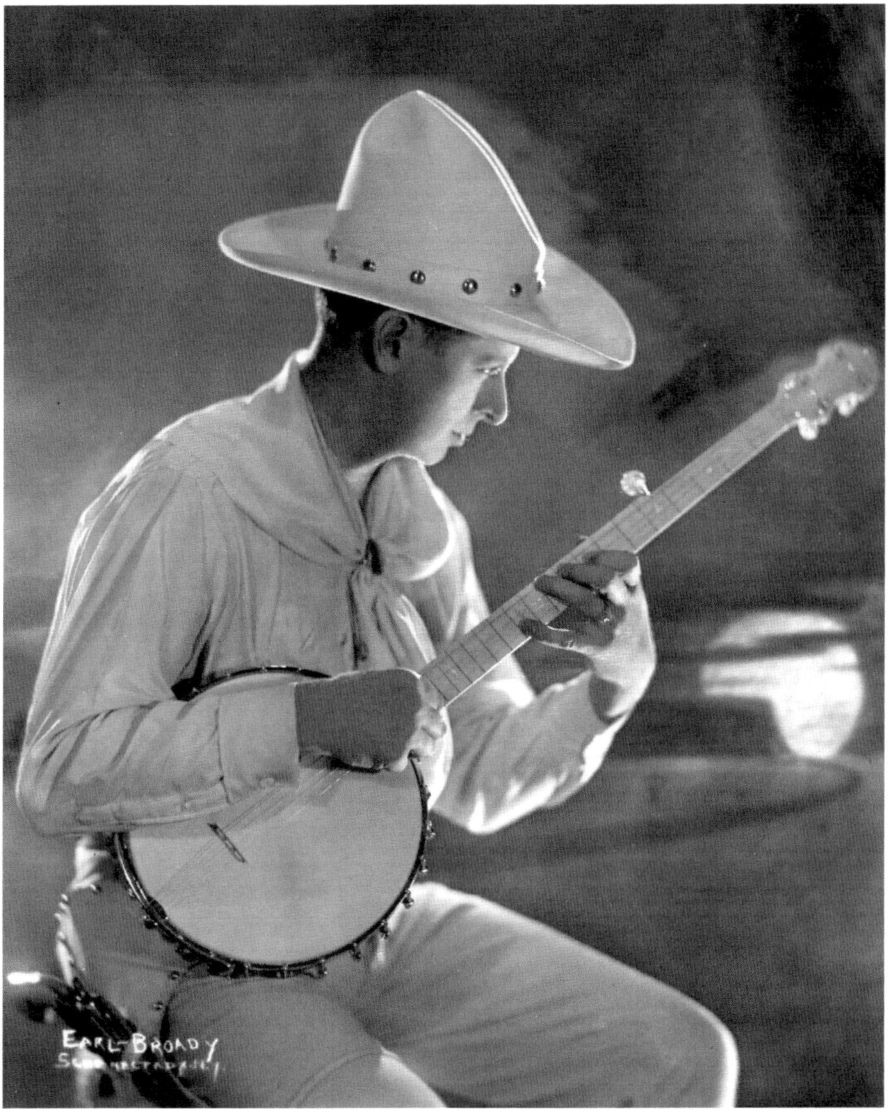

Vaudeville musician Raymond Montana was known on the circuit as Montana the Cowboy Banjoist. © *Montana family*.

traveling with their vaudeville parents, Ruth's crib was a pillow placed in the drawer of a dresser.

Raymond was the top banjoist in the country and was reported to have been the world's highest-paid banjo player. He strongly believed in self-discipline and practiced over five hours a day. His hard work paid off, as can be seen in the words written by the editor of *Metronome* when describing Raymond's onstage presence:

> *Everyone knows Montana, the celebrated cowboy banjoist. Montana is called "the white cowboy" throughout the country. He has an ideal personality for vaudeville and motion picture theatre work, owing to his splendid presence and the fact that he is considered the most richly dressed man in the whole show game. He is a great performer on the banjo and has played practically every big theatre circuit throughout the whole world.*[2]

By the spring of 1920, another little Coleman was on the way. When the tour ended for the season, the family looked forward to settling down and rented a small cottage in Stockton, California. It was in that cottage, reportedly delivered by an Indian squaw, that Robert William Coleman was born on October 23, 1920. October, with all its celebrations, had become a truly special month for the family. Raymond and Roberta were thankful to have been blessed with a healthy little boy; however, what they didn't know was that their newborn baby boy would someday grow up to be one of the world's greatest cartoonists.

Chapter 2

Dust Off the Trunk

Hailed as the world's greatest banjoist, Montana strummed his way into the hearts of his listeners Monday, offering a varied selection and climaxing his program with the introduction of his small daughter and still smaller son. The two children proved just as great a hit as their father and wound up the act in fine fashion.

—Seattle Union Record, *March 28, 1926*

With the birth of Bobby Coleman, Raymond and Roberta decided it would be best to stay in one place for several years. All traveling stopped, and Raymond formed a jazz band locally in order to satisfy his desire to play music. However, early in 1923, when the children were old enough to travel, he began to hanker for the days of old when he toured as a performer. He proclaimed it was time for the family to dust off the trunk, create a new vaudeville routine and rejoin the circuit. This time, they were known simply as the Montanas, and when traveling, it was little Bobby who used the dresser drawer as a crib. Ruth gladly gave up the drawer in favor of a small cot.

Raymond's banjo routine was still in high demand, and the Pantages theaters of the West eagerly added the Montanas to their rosters in September 1923. The circuit worked its way eastward, ending the season in New England the following June. When the family was not performing, using the last name of Coleman seemed to continually clash with the well-known name they used on stage. Thoughts of an official name change began

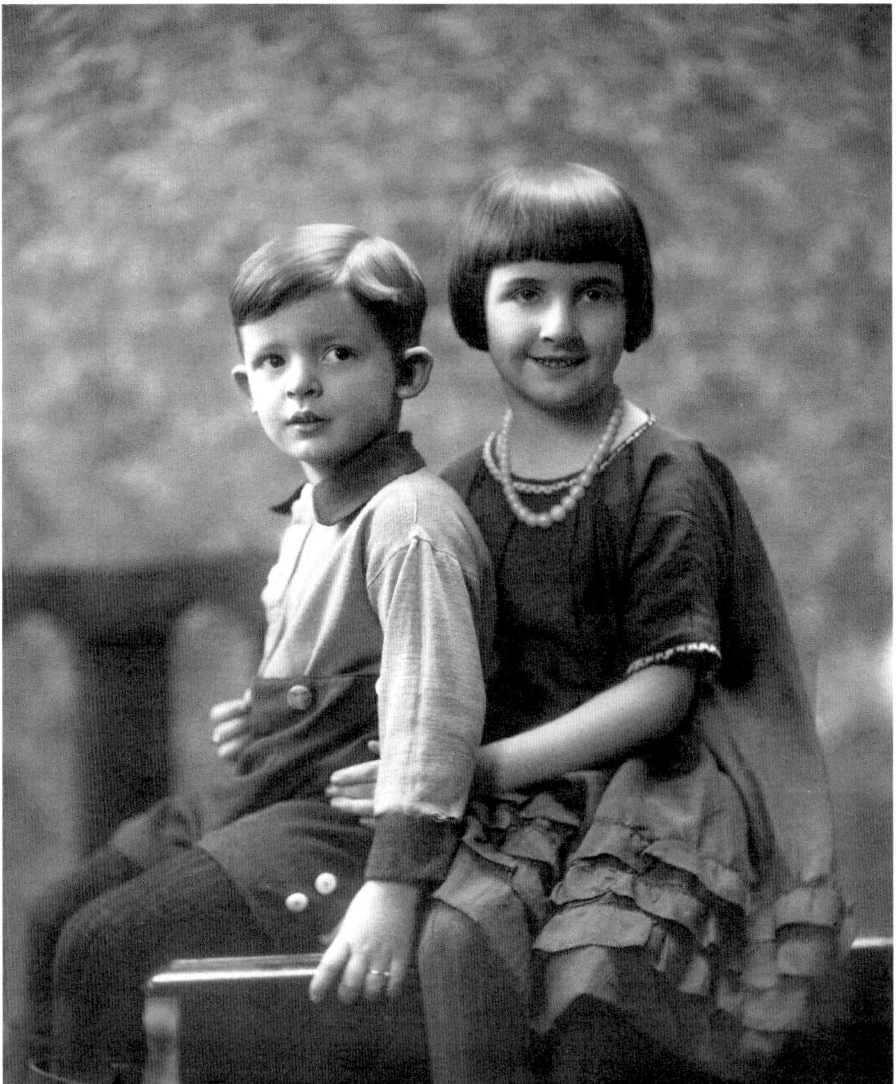

Bobby and Ruth Montana, circa 1925. © *Montana family*.

to swirl through their minds; however, it would be another few years before the Colemans would pursue changing the family name permanently.

During their summer break in 1924, the Colemans stayed with vaudeville friends who vacationed each year in New Hampshire. It was then that Raymond and Roberta discovered the small but beautiful town of Meredith, which overlooks the spectacular Lake Winnipesaukee, the state's largest. In an instant, they felt a connection to the town and fell in love with it.

It was easy to be enchanted with Meredith; the history of it holds its own charm. The community's first settlers were farmers drawn to the area by some of the most fertile soil in the state. Farming there was easy, but the town's village had notable water sites, making it the focus of cotton and linen manufacturers, and Meredith quickly became known for its mills.

When the Colemans arrived, the shorelines of all five of the lakes located in town saw seasonal waterfront cottages being built one after another, and the town focused on catering to periodic tourists.[3] It was the farming portion of the town's history that fascinated Raymond the most, and he insisted on purchasing a small farm for the family to utilize during their vacations. Within a few weeks, they had located a house with approximately ten acres of land on Meredith Neck, and their little paradise became known as Montana Gardens. The purchase of a thirty-five-foot boat to be used to sail the waters of Lake Winnipesaukee was the icing on the cake for the Coleman family. They appropriately named her the *Banjo Queen*.

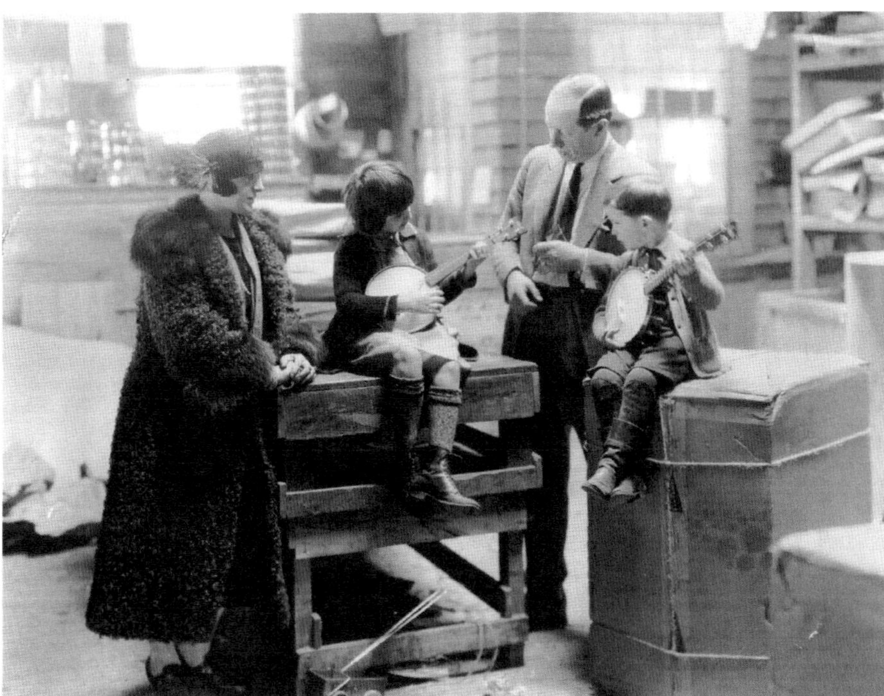

Raymond and Roberta Montana, along with their children, traveled the world as a vaudeville act. © *Montana family*.

The following summer, in 1925, Ruth and Bobby were old enough for Roberta to teach them a short, easy dance routine, and Raymond gave them instruction on how to properly harmonize. When the family returned to vaudeville in September, the children became the grand finishing touch to Raymond's act, and they were an instant hit with adoring audiences everywhere. Being young performers, the siblings were taught that when in public, any anger or frustration was always kept private. Bob later recalled how difficult this sometimes was, saying, "I even had to smile while my sister twisted my arm behind my back. She did this quite often if I didn't behave or do what she wanted."[4]

Those early years were happy and busy times. The days and months were filled with performing, traveling and mingling with large numbers of people, the latter providing endless entertainment for young Bobby. One of his favorite things to do when not performing was to sit backstage, watch and listen to the comedy routines of some of the most brilliant performers of vaudeville. Undoubtedly, this had a great influence on his sense of humor and his ability to find the comical side to every situation in life.

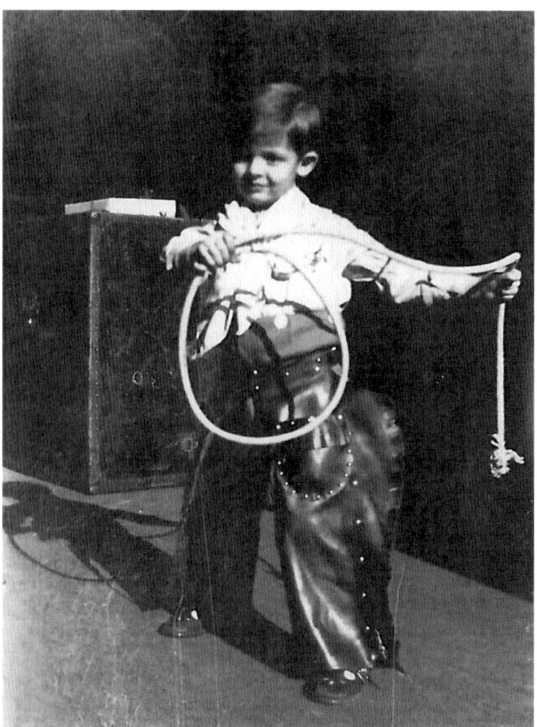

After mastering rope tricks, Bobby became part of his father's vaudeville act. © *Montana family*.

By the time Bobby turned six in 1926, Raymond had purchased his son a lariat and taught him rope tricks. Yet he would always gravitate back to what he liked best: his drawing pads and pencils. Bobby, like his father before him, had already decided what he wanted to do with his life at an early age. He declared that he wanted to be a cartoonist. His desire and ability to draw comics did not go unnoticed. When the renowned cartoonist Fay King saw some of his drawings, she predicted that the young lad would someday become a great artist.[5]

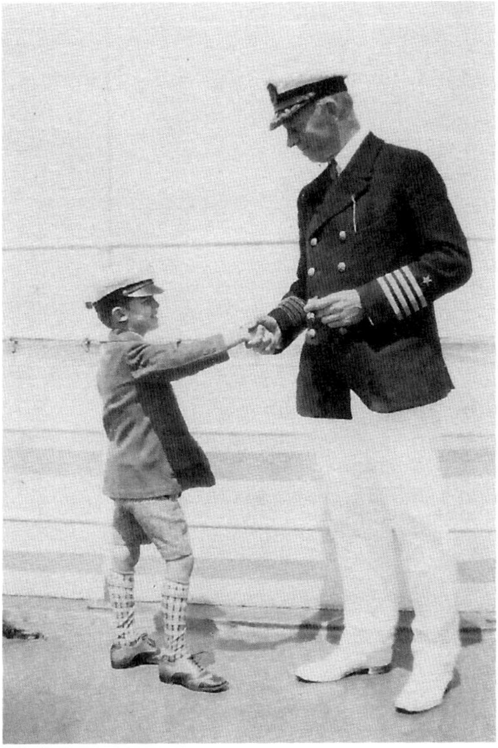

Bobby shakes hands with Captain George Fried aboard the USS *President Roosevelt*. © *Montana family*.

In July 1927, the family set sail for England aboard the USS *President Roosevelt* after Raymond had secured a tour overseas. But first, the family agreed that this was an opportune time to have their name change legalized in order to avoid any confusion between their stage name and the name that appeared on their passports. The Coleman name was left behind forever, and Montana became the name they carried into the future.

Once in England, Raymond played in numerous theaters, beginning at the Holborn Empire Theater in London. At the end of August, the tour drew to a close at Scotland's Glasgow Pavilion. The summer tour had been an enormous success and was the crowning glory of Raymond's musical career. As for Bobby, he had been so taken by the luxurious ship they traveled on that it became his most memorable part of the trip.

In the late 1920s, America's economy was careening out of control, and the carefree and exciting lifestyle of the Montanas was about to undergo abrupt and startling changes. Vaudeville was dying, and the Roaring Twenties were coming to an end. Advances in technology were underway, and the public had become fascinated with the new talking pictures. After the crash of the stock market in 1929, vaudeville was gone forever and became only a page in America's history.

Raymond suddenly went from being a superstar to a man without steady employment. In 1930, the family headed for Meredith to live and work on their farm. Assisted by their gardener, they grew all their own produce and sold the excess in town. To supplement their income, Raymond jumped at the chance to perform at larger theaters that still wanted or could afford

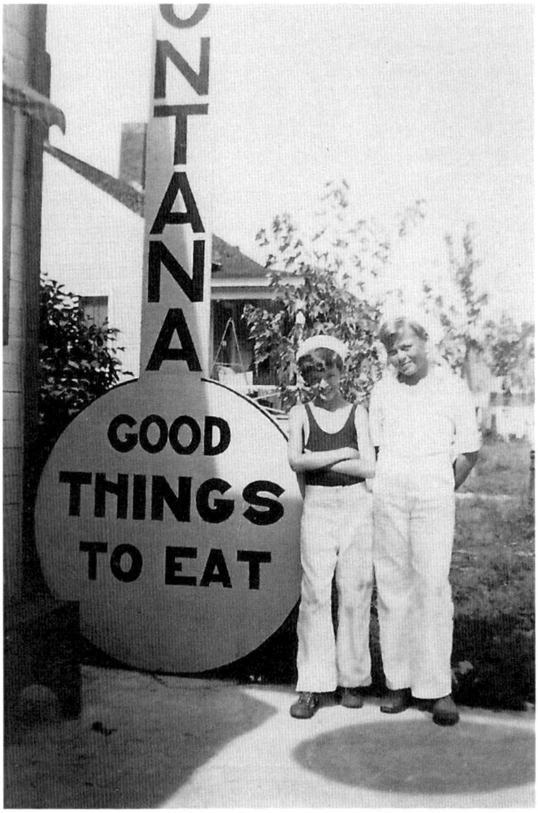

Bobby (left) stands in front of his family's restaurant in Meredith. © *Montana family*.

vaudeville-type acts. There was one big difference: his routine was scheduled after the main event—the movie.

Back home, Ruth and Bobby adjusted well to living in one place even though their new lifestyle was far different than the one they had known previously. The Montana children had been world travelers, and by the time Bobby turned eight, the family had visited all forty-eight states, as well as England and Scotland. Their education was a family affair, with Roberta and Raymond taking time to teach them their lessons in between traveling and performing. That fall, the Montana children did something they had never done before: they attended their first full year in a public school.

In 1931, the nation's economic woes continued, and the Montanas had even less money. Yet Raymond and Roberta opened a restaurant in town called Montana's. Roberta was a talented cook and skillfully used the food they produced on their farm to cook up delicious meals and desserts. Ruth was old enough to be a waitress and called upon her friend Hazel Bickford to work with her. Raymond felt fortunate to have found another outlet for his banjo playing. When he wasn't handling the business end of the restaurant, he was out among the patrons entertaining them.

Bobby was too young to work, but there were people of considerable importance entering his life that would later play a large part in shaping it. One was Harold O. Whitney, a wealthy summer resident of Meredith who hailed from Watertown, Massachusetts. A friend of Raymond's, Harold would often stop by the restaurant for a visit with the family. When everyone was busy,

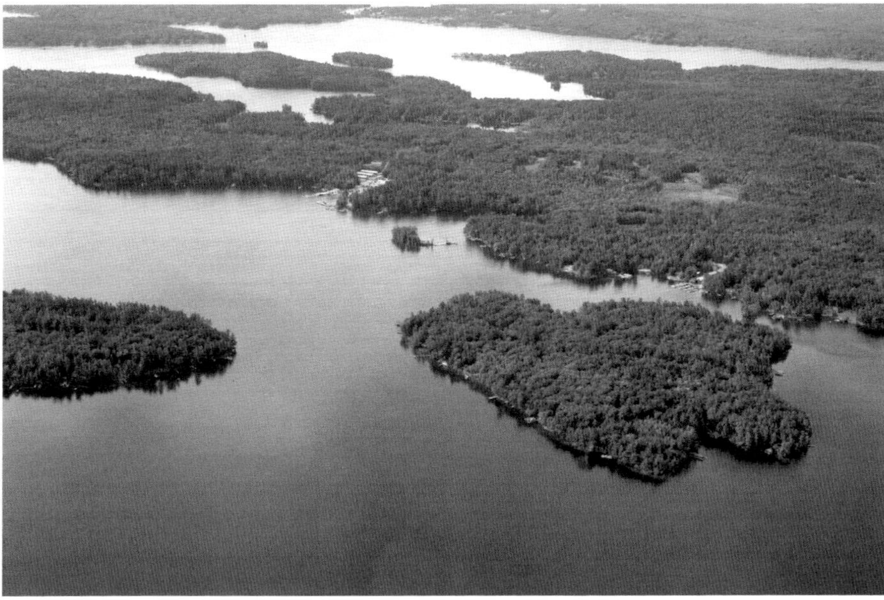

Pine Island (center right) was the location of the summer home of millionaire H.O. Whitney. Meredith Neck is located behind the island. *Photo by Harrison Haas.*

he would help entertain Bobby by bringing him out to the Whitney summer camp on Pine Island, just off the shore of Meredith Neck. Harold quickly became impressed with the boy's artistic talent and gave him a large wooden paint box as a gift. It was the only paint box Bobby would ever own.

As for the restaurant, it had been a tough year, and it was struggling. As the Depression deepened in 1932, the Montanas' world collapsed. They were forced to close the restaurant, and they lost their beloved farm. Selling everything they could, they headed south to Boston. Miraculously, Raymond managed to rent a building on the Shubert Theater Alley. The ever-optimistic Montana family put their all into a new restaurant they called the Rancho. A simple western theme was used for the décor, and Bobby was delighted to have been asked to paint western murals on the walls.

Trying to run a new restaurant in a busy metropolitan area did not help the Montanas regain a stable footing. They were living in a hotel, all in one room. When Thanksgiving Day arrived, a meal of salami and bread was what they faced for a holiday meal. Their luck changed when friends G. Laurence Hall and his wife, Margaret Pope, stopped by to check in on the family's new venture. The well-to-do couple took the Montanas out for a proper Thanksgiving celebration. The salami and bread would wait for another time.

Laurence, an electrical engineer and lecturer at the Massachusetts Institute of Technology, had a great love for the theater. Not far from the Lenox Hotel in Boston, where he and Margaret lived, Laurence kept a studio. There he experimented with changing theater costumes and scenery by using ultraviolet light combined with the use of fluorescent paint. Laurence was well aware of Bobby's artist talents and regularly put them to good use. The Halls became close family friends of the Montanas, and they were two of the young boy's favorite people. Both his father and Laurence encouraged Bobby to join the Masons, which he did when he joined the Order of DeMolay.

Laurence lent Raymond money to buy the necessary items to properly get the Rancho up and running. This time, the entire family was involved with running the restaurant. Bobby was put to work as a busboy, Ruth checked in hats, Roberta was the perfect hostess and, of course, the restaurant was not complete without Raymond's banjo routine providing the entertainment. Prohibition strongly challenged the establishment, but at the end of 1933 when the law was repealed, the Rancho quickly became a popular nightclub and began making a good profit.

Bobby honed his artist skills and gained valuable experience by drawing caricatures of the patrons. Harold Whitney worked to make sure Bobby attended art lessons, first at Exeter Art School and then with the Boston Museum of Fine Arts. He also showed Bobby's artwork to Mr. Lodge of the Boston Lodges, who then hired the aspiring artist to paint murals with a nautical theme on the walls of his basement.

It seemed as if the Montanas' luck had turned, and they were on their way to again being highly successful. Gone were the days of the struggle and the financial hardship of the last few years. Throughout it all, they had each other to lean on and knew that no matter how difficult life became, they would always be there for each other.

Chapter 3

I Want to Be an Artist

"Pa died August 20, 1935." Those were some of the first words Bob Montana wrote in his high school diary, which he began keeping in January 1937. His father's death was the single most tragic event in his life. For a family that had struggled through the turmoil of the Depression and was beginning to see brighter days, Raymond's death brought about swift, sad and permanent changes to each of their lives. Bob remained true to what he had been taught: personal sadness and frustration should always remain private and never be shown in public.

The details of Raymond's life during the months leading up to his death are few and simple. As 1935 began to unfold, life for the Montanas continued to improve with the success of the Rancho. The family missed their farm on Meredith Neck, especially the water activities they had enjoyed on Lake Winnipesaukee. Being so rooted in Boston made it impossible for them to visit Meredith, so in July, Raymond purchased a camp on Pillings Pond in Lynnfield, Massachusetts. Bob spent most of his spare time in the lake with his faithful companion, an adopted terrier named Jikky.

Each weekend during the summer, the family delighted in and relaxed at their new camp. On August 20, the Montana children were in the lake swimming with their father, as they had throughout the swimming season. By the end of the day, their world would be turned upside down. Raymond suffered a heart attack while on the beach and collapsed. His family watched helplessly, and by the time a doctor arrived, it was too late. Montana the Cowboy Banjoist, the world's greatest banjo player, had died at the age of fifty-five.

In an instant, life's challenges seemed insurmountable, yet the family tried to return to the life they knew before Raymond's death. Roberta attempted to stay focused on running the Rancho, but the next few months were intensely difficult for a variety of reasons. Raymond's show had been extremely popular and drew in customers. With him not there, business began to dwindle. Friends of the family tried to help in any way possible, but the restaurant continued to lose money. Friend Harold Rodman, an employee of a local costume and scenery company, would often stop by at night to offer assistance, as some of the male patrons were often a challenge.

Laurence Hall helped Bob get through the rough months of the fall, and visits to Laurence's studio helped immensely. Laurence was aware that it was a critical time for stability and became a father figure to the young man. He advised Bob to stay in DeMolay. Not only did he stay in it, but by November, he had received his first and second degrees.

Yet life had still more changes and upheaval in store. In November, Ruth married her long-time boyfriend. The newlyweds settled down on Pillings Pond, just a stone's throw away from the camp where Raymond had died. Roberta became more and more lonely, and Bob found it incredibly difficult to be at the Rancho. He was heartbroken over the death of his father, and the restaurant only offered painful reminders of all that he had lost. Too discouraged and too tired to keep the struggling restaurant open, Roberta closed it shortly after Christmas.

The New Year brought marriage for Roberta and Harold Rodman. They were married on January 25, 1936, and immediately moved to Haverhill, Massachusetts. Bob was able to finally graduate that June from Bradford Grammar School and was anxiously looking forward to attending high school in Haverhill. After the events of the last year, he needed to simply focus on being a teenager. He spent an uneventful and fairly relaxing summer with Ruth at Pillings Pond and started as a student at Haverhill High School about the same time as the arrival of his stepsister, Georgie. Despite having to adjust to the antics of a new baby, Bob jumped into high school life with all the energy and optimism of a typical teenage boy. He drew cartoons for the school paper, *Brown & Gold*; joined the swimming team; and painted scenery for plays. He loved to dance and attended as many school dances as his hectic schedule allowed. Bob always referred to his high school years as the best in his life, and with good reason—he was leading a full life. He was busy, he was making friends and he was happy.

At times, Bob's personal life outside of high school was even busier. When Harold needed help with scenery and posters for the Hooker Howe Co.,

Bob would pitch in. So that he could play golf for free, he caddied at the Haverhill Country Club. He was fascinated with movies, an interest that began during vaudeville, when silent movies were only one act. Boston was still an attraction, as the Halls lived there, and Bob would often work at Laurence's studio when visiting. He would also go to DeMolay, as he was producing *Gavel*, the organization's paper.

During two of his high school years, Bob kept a personal diary that contains an endearing collection of entries showing his cartooning style and humor beginning to blossom. As much as he described his life and the world around him with words, he never failed to illustrate those entries. The diary is evidence that Bob was a typical teenager with the same hopes and frustrations as his classmates. In other ways, however, he was very different; he possessed extraordinary talents for a high school student. As remarkable is a caricature he drew of himself in one of the entries. That drawing was the perfect prototype for his future comic character, Archie. Plaid pants, saddle shoes and a toothy grin, Bob—or rather, Archie—walked across a

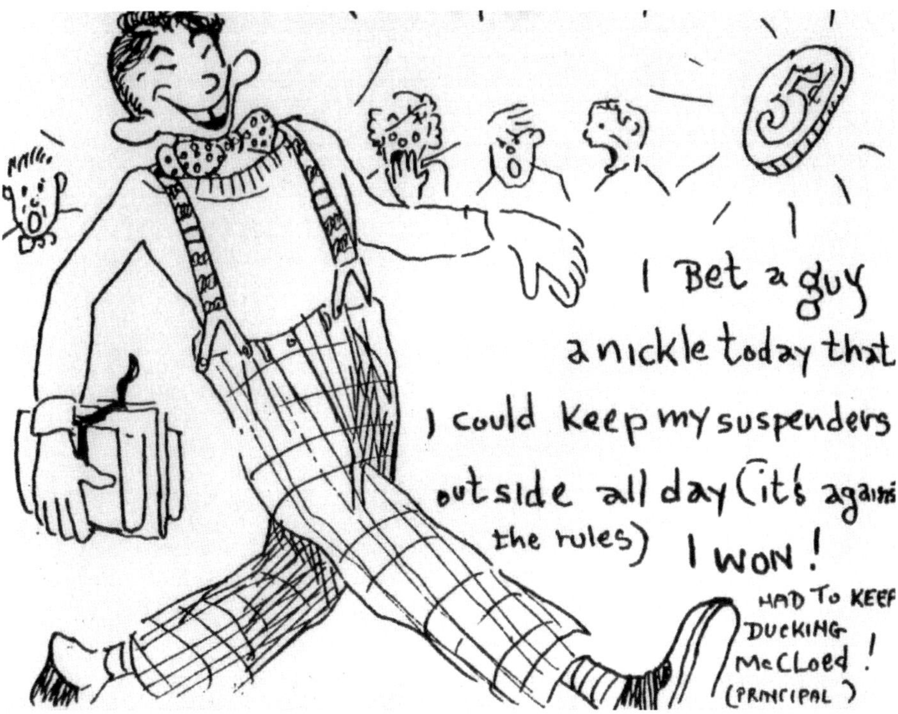

The illustrations in Bob's high school diary included this image of an Archie-like character in a 1938 entry. © *Montana family*.

page in his diary. It would be a few years before he would be drawing the *Archie* comic for a living, and he first needed to graduate from high school.

Bob spent the first three years of high school in Haverhill, but more changes appeared on the horizon. During his freshman year, Ruth came home to live after her marriage had dissolved. During the summer of 1939, Harold was hired by a company in Manchester, New Hampshire, forcing Bob to spend his senior year at Manchester High School. This was a tremendous disappointment since he had planned on graduating from Haverhill High. Nevertheless, he made the best of it. In the fall, he enrolled in Manchester Central High School, where he studied art with Mr. Ryder, the teacher Bob credited with steering

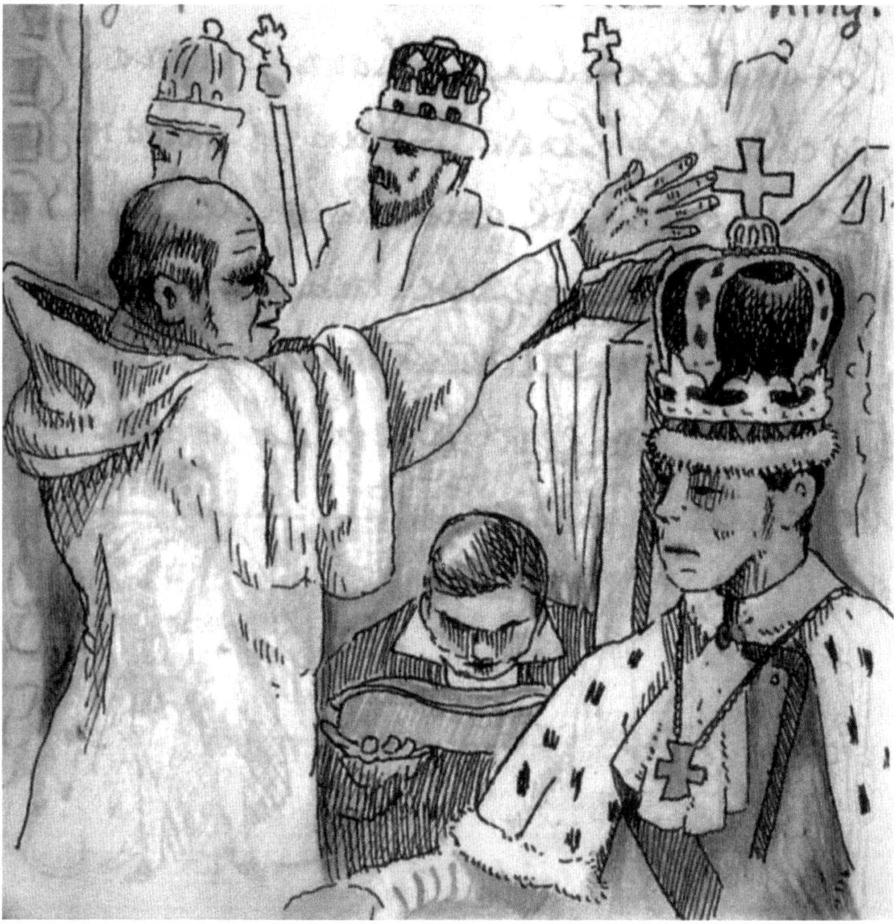

Diary entries that detailed Bob's personal life, as well as world events, included rich, detailed illustrations. © *Montana family*.

him toward a career in art. Any strenuous activities were off-limits, since it was discovered that he had developed a slight heart murmur. He was allowed to join the fencing team and was the only member of the team that competed in his favorite Archie-style saddle shoes. Golf was still of great interest to him, and he joined the caddies golf team at the Bedford Country Club.

A childhood spent in vaudeville inspired him to join the drama club, not only to act in plays but also to design and paint scenery. Scenes were often hurriedly painted during study hall, but he learned the hard way that haste makes waste and that it could instantaneously throw the entire school into an uproar. Just prior to a dress rehearsal, Bob arrived on stage and planned to quickly finish painting the scenery. However, he found that the paintbrushes were hidden out of reach, locked inside a grill on the electrical box that controlled the lighting for the stage. One brush was all he needed, so he used a wire coat hanger during his attempt to hook the brush. Suddenly, there was a bright flash, and he was thrown to the floor. He had short-circuited the entire electrical system of the building, and the school was in total darkness. The trouble he was in with the school officials paled in comparison to the trouble he was in with the girls in the cooking class. Their cakes were baking in the ovens when he knocked out the electricity. To say the girls were upset with him when their cakes fell is an understatement, and the fact that he was still alive after nearly being electrocuted didn't seem to matter much to them.

Bob got into a few scrapes here and there in his personal life as well. He was continually looking for ways to earn money with his artistic talents, and he quickly became successful at designing, painting and selling greeting cards. The local newspaper in Manchester would often include some of his panel cartoons. Sign painting proved to be more of a challenge, and his brave venture into this specialty ended rather suddenly. A local company hired him to design and paint a logo on the sides of their truck. The project progressed well until he had to flip the logo for the opposite side of the vehicle, which didn't fit when reversed. Horrified, he cut his losses and immediately retired from the sign-painting business.

Bob survived his sometimes–hair-raising teenage adventures and graduated from high school in 1940. The last entry in his diary shows his apprehension about the war being fought in Europe. He was well aware of the seriousness of what was happening on foreign soils. Yet with the youthful optimism of a teenager, he wrote that he hoped that the United States would stay out of the war. His desire was not to become a soldier. He had one goal in life, which he firmly stated in his diary: "I want to be an artist."

The summer after graduation, Bob worked long hours selling hot dogs at an amusement park and saved as much money as possible, tucking it

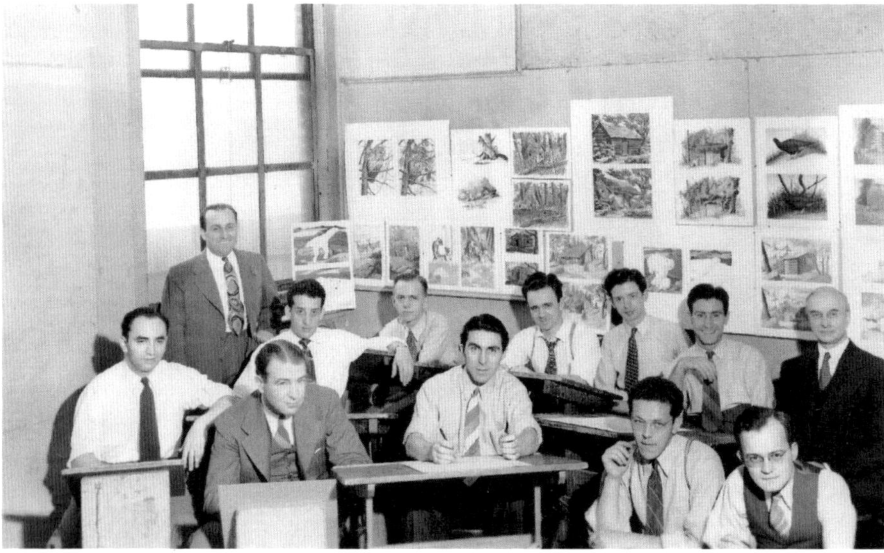

Bob (back row, third from right) poses with his class at the Phoenix Art Institute. © *Montana family*.

away for art school. His plan was to save approximately $200 and leave in late August to attend art school in New York City. After saving all summer, additional funds were needed, so Roberta, Ruth and the Halls chipped in enough money to help him get on his way.

As Bob was about to board the bus headed to the city, Roberta made a sudden but not surprising decision. Her marriage to Harold had completely fallen apart, and she was eager to start a new life in a different place. Her sister, Olga, lived in Brooklyn with her family, so the twosome lived with her until they were able to secure a small apartment in Coney Island.

Bob's mission and goal was to find the right art school in the city. He applied to his number-one choice, the Phoenix Art Institute, and was accepted at once. His instructor was to be Franklyn Booth, a popular and well-known illustrator, and Bob anxiously waited for the first day of classes. He temporarily set aside his dream of becoming a cartoonist and focused on becoming an illustrator. In an illustrated letter to Margaret and Laurence Hall dated September 19, 1940, he told of life in New York City and how much he enjoyed his classes at school. The ten-minute breaks in class were never utilized by the eager student, and his words tell of his elation at being immersed in art: "I still don't get enough—it's so good to be in art school."

Chapter 4

We Call Him Archie Montana

Everything that happens to Archie happened to me in school...there's one great difference. Archie always gets out of his troubles in the end, but it seems to me that I was always stuck. Guess I didn't have a Jughead to get me out of tight places.
—Bob Montana, September 1946

While a student at the Phoenix Art School in New York City, Bob Montana happily focused on honing his techniques in illustration and worked selling newspapers and as a busboy. Ruth joined him and their mother that fall, and the trio rented an apartment together on Twenty-fourth Street. Bob's schedule allowed him time to work on his portfolio, and he felt it was the appropriate time to look for a job as an illustrator. The field offered few jobs, and he soon began to apply for a variety of positions in the art field.

After working for a short time at Fox Comics drawing cartoons, a friend mentioned to him that Parents Inc. was actively looking to hire a cartoonist for their comic book *True*. After applying, he was hired immediately and then hailed as the company's newest cartoonist. His background had given him the ability to draw the humor he observed in life, and that skill was about to come in handy. Between classes at Phoenix, working for *True* and for Rube Goldberg, he also set aside time to develop his own comic strip, but attempts to market it to publishers were unsuccessful.[6]

Bob's artistic genius, however, was about to transform American comics, as well as his entire life. He was hired by MLJ Magazines, and the company was in the process of searching for new, innovative ideas for its comics. Bob

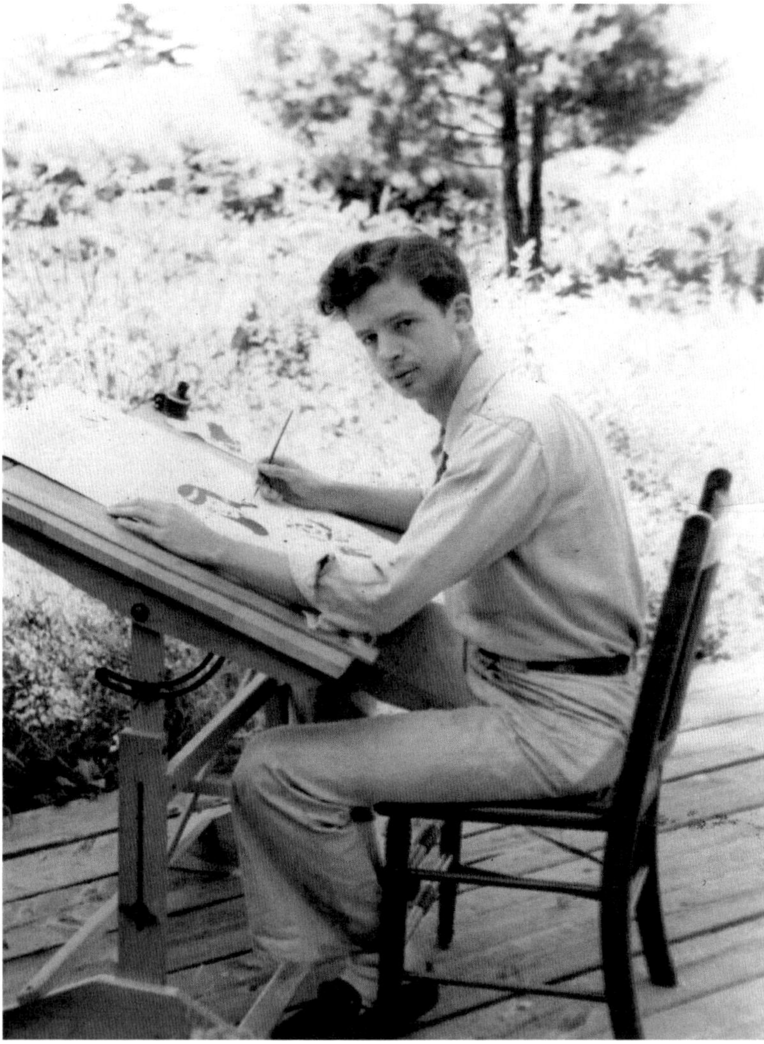

Bob Montana drawing the first *Archie* comic book in 1942 on the shore of Meredith's Lake Waukewan. © *Montana family*.

was asked to work on a storyline that involved teenagers and high school life. It was a dream assignment since those years had been his favorite. The biggest challenge he faced was transforming his ideas and stories into comic format and then writing the proper comic dialogue to accompany them. Harry Shorten, then-editor of MLJ, became Bob's mentor in this area. Creating humorous dialogue wasn't a challenge for Bob; it came naturally.

The comic Bob presented to his supervisors at MLJ featured the teenage adventures of two girls and two boys. He modeled the main character, Archie, after himself and his sometimes-wild high school episodes. Beautiful Veronica Lodge was a blend of actress Veronica Lake and the Boston Lodges, and Betty was given the name of a former girlfriend. Jughead, Archie's loyal friend throughout, was a skillful concoction of a number of Bob's high school friends.[7]

In the fall of 1941, Bob drew the first four-page *Archie* comic, which appeared in the November issue of Pep Comics. Throughout the winter and the following spring, additional *Archie* comics appeared regularly in Pep or Jackpot comic books. With the rapidly increasing popularity of Archie, it was clear that the market could easily support a comic book dedicated exclusively to the teenagers of the fictional Riverdale High. That summer, Bob rented a camp on Lake Waukewan in Meredith, New Hampshire, and drew the first Archie comic book, called *The Mirth of a Nation*. When the stories went to the printers in the fall, Bob, at the tender age of twenty-one, became the youngest top cartoonist in American history. The record-setting young man remained humble, and while still employed by MLJ, he enlisted in the army.

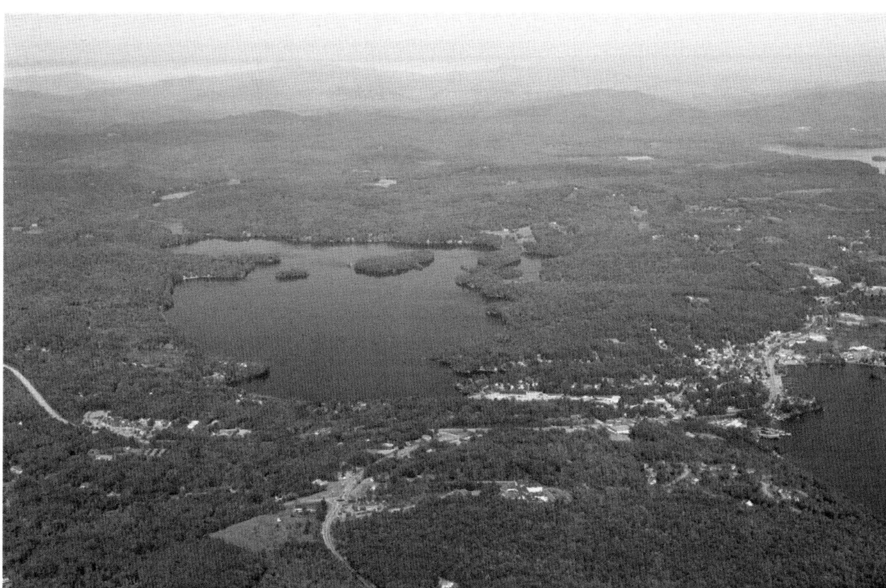

Lake Waukewan with Meredith Village and Meredith Bay on the right. *Photo by Harrison Haas.*

Bob became a dedicated member of the nation's military, and his greatest difficulty was finding the time to draw and write *Archie* stories. It was a tough juggling act, and soon other cartoonists at MLJ were trained to draw the characters when Bob could not. He had only one request: that the cartoonists who did draw for *Archie* not sign their names to any work that included his characters.

Bob's years in the army were spent stateside, initially as a filmstrip artist at the Signal Corps Photographic Center located within the Astoria Film Studio on Long Island, New York. Later, he found himself at the U.S. Air Corps at Drew Field after a dispatcher mistakenly directed him to board the wrong train during a transfer. He was assigned to a new squadron, which was scheduled to depart for England. Fortunately, Bob's paperwork detailing the dispatcher's mistake arrived shortly before he set sail. The cartoonist returned to the Signal Corps and was assigned to the Publications Agency at Fort Monmouth, New Jersey. The transfer was permanent, and he remained there until his discharge. His duties included mostly technical work, but the army kept him busy drawing cartoons for the Signal Corps newsletter. Additionally, he drew a large number of greeting cards for visiting dignitaries, earning him the nickname "Hallmark."

Archie, in the meantime, had become a smashing success. The enormous popularity of the comic book fueled the creation of a syndicated comic strip that appeared in newspapers nationwide. The workload of drawing both the *Archie* comic books and a daily strip for the papers could never be done by just one man. Bob knew he could handle drawing the comic strip himself, so he agreed to let other artists handle the comic book. In the fall of 1945, he signed a contract with McClure Syndicate and began drawing *Archie* in comic-strip format in November. It first appeared in newspapers on February 6, 1946, two weeks before his official discharge from the army.

MLJ knew it had hit the jackpot. *Archie*, no matter what the format, spelled success for the company, and Bob Montana, the man who created it, would forever be known as one of America's finest cartoonists. The company introduced him to its readers in an article describing Bob as being so much like the lovable Archie that the two were virtually inseparable:

> *You're sure you don't know anyone named Bob Montana...and yet you've got the sneaking feeling that you've seen the face before. Where, you ask yourself, biting your nails and beating your head against the wall, have I seen that guy before?*

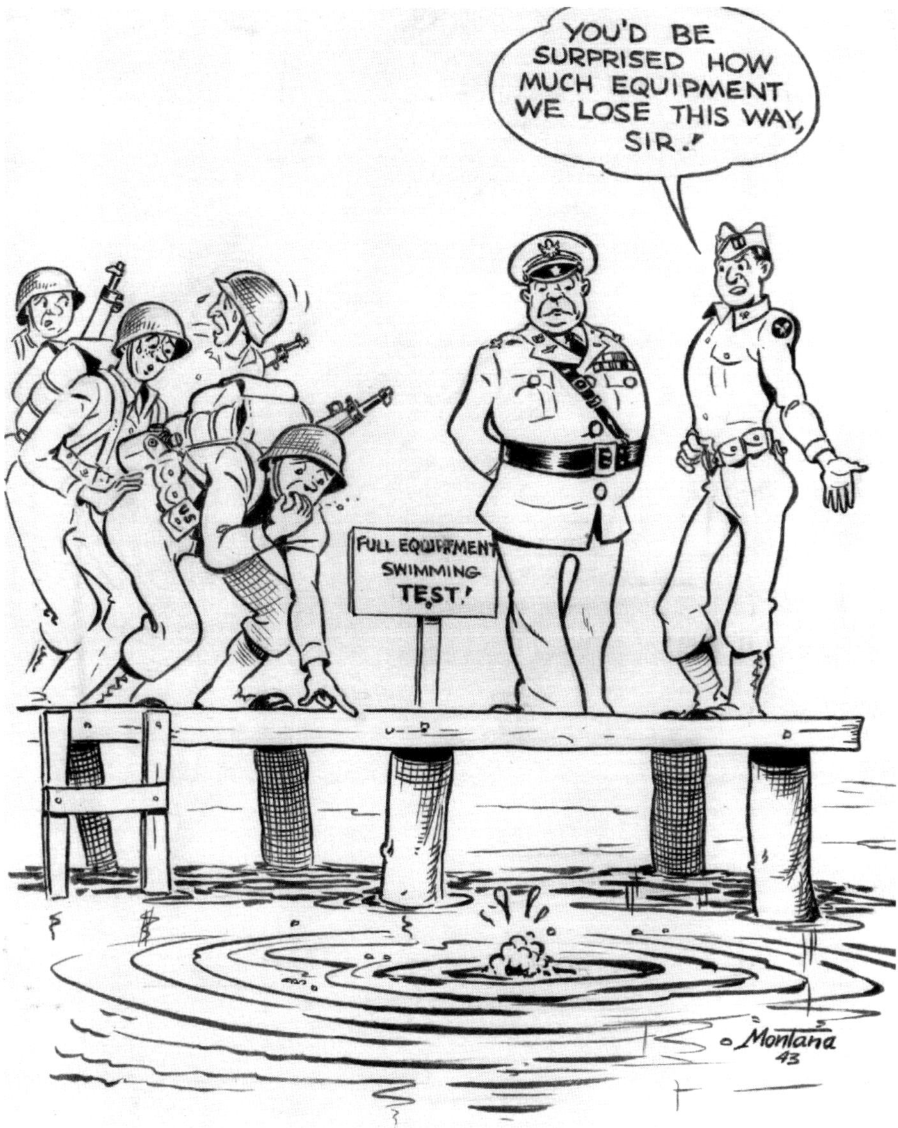

While in the army, Bob created comics for the Signal Corps newsletter. © *Montana family*.

I'll answer that question. You've seen the guy before in every Archie *strip you've ever read—seen him in every drawing of Archie. For Bob Montana has the unconscious habit of putting himself into his drawings, and there is no getting away from it. Up here at MLJ, we call him Archie Montana.*

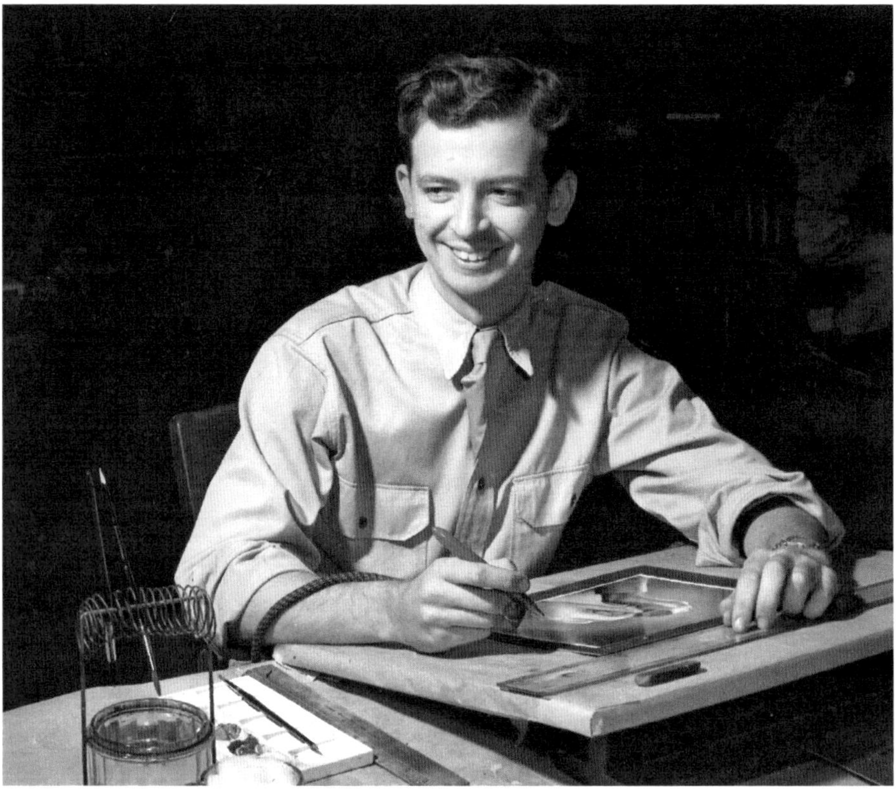

Smiling army staff sergeant Bob Montana looking quite like Archie. © *Montana family*.

> *Naturally, you can't tell as well from the drawings as you could, if for example, you worked with the guy...because a drawing can catch only one pose—only one emotion. But I've seen the guy in all moods, and I know. I've seen him hilarious over some idea for his next* Archie *strip, and I've seen him plenty sore when ideas didn't want to come. And in every movement, every gesture, the guy is Archie. I'll tell you all I know about him. Then, if you really want to find out what he's like, follow his comic strip.*[8]

Archie had become such a big seller that MLJ Magazines reorganized and became known as Archie Comics Publications Inc. Still, Bob's choice to focus on the comic strip was prudent planning, and there was an important reason he made it. He was getting married. While in the service, he met Peggy Wherett, a native of New Jersey. The strikingly beautiful young woman was a model and a secretary working at Fort Monmouth where

Bob had been stationed. Peggy, known to most as Peg, described those early days with the cartoonist:

> *Bob Montana and I met in January 1945 when we worked together at the Publications Agency at Fort Monmouth in New Jersey. Bob was a staff sergeant in the art department, and I was a civil service secretary for his captain. Bob was a very active, sociable but quiet person who, besides his regular work, put in extra hours on the* Archie *stories, greeting cards for visiting dignitaries and cartoons for the* Fort Monmouth News.
>
> *Whenever Bob had a weekend pass, we would go into New York City to the art museums, ballet or the theater, which was so much a part of this man. He proposed in the Astor Lounge after attending the Broadway musical* Carousel.
>
> *In February 1946, Bob was discharged from the army, and Archie was launched into the newspaper world. On April 13, Bob and I were married, and after our honeymoon, we headed for Meredith, New Hampshire, and stayed in the same camp where the first* Archie *comic book was drawn.*
>
> *I fell in love with Bob's little New England town. He showed me the farm where his family rested and played every summer after trouping the vaudeville circuit from September until June. Bob introduced me to family friends, including Mr. H.O. Whitney, who was H.O. Pittney in an early newspaper story. In the spring of 1947, we bought our own camp on Lake Winnipesaukee.*[9]

As a married man, Bob knew where he wanted to live and raise a family, and it wasn't in New York City. His childhood hometown of Meredith was his first and only choice. He wisely created a storyline that would send the characters in *Archie* to New Hampshire. It entailed a carefully planned transition, one that fans could understand and one that could be accomplished swiftly and smoothly. McClure Syndicate issued a press release to explain the transition:

> *Bob Montana, who draws the famous* Archie *comic strip, and his bride are honeymooning at Camp Ash on Lake Waukewan, New Hampshire.*
>
> *Like other comic artists, Montana has to turn out a comic strip a day, even on his honeymoon. However, he hit upon an idea to simplify his work and give him more time for attention to his bride. He endowed the* Archie *story with a new plot which takes his characters to New Hampshire for the summer.*

> *In this new story, the beautiful and rich Veronica invites Archie's faithful girlfriend, Betty, to be her guest at a New Hampshire camp. Betty doesn't want to be separated from Archie, and so when a store announces that it will give a chance of a vacation in New Hampshire with each compass sold, Betty spends all her savings for compasses and puts Archie's name on each chance. Archie and his pal Jughead win, and so all of his principal characters are off to Lake Winnipesaukee.*
>
> *This will simplify Montana's work, because he can use the lakes and scenery of the region for his backgrounds, and he plans to draw heavily from life as he sees it in New Hampshire summer camps. As a consequence, some residents and summer visitors may find themselves in the funny papers!*
>
> *Montana considers himself a New Englander. Since Montana's strip appears in newspapers from coast to coast, the beauties and the lure of New Hampshire's lakes and woods will be widely publicized through Archie's adventures this summer.*[10]

On July 8, 1946, the contest saga involving Betty and the compasses began, and Archie, Jughead, Veronica and Betty soon headed to Lake Winnipesaukee for their summer vacation. Fans following the strip spent a humorous summer with Archie and his three pals, with the vacation theme coming to a close on September 2, 1946. It was then back to school for the students of Riverdale High.

In the series of strips from that summer, Bob had carefully placed some important names and people within it. He illustrated the steepness of Ladd Hill in Meredith by having Archie and Jughead drive down the hill, follow the road and drive right into the lake. His father-in-law, Mr. Wherett, was included and offered a free boat to Archie and Jughead for their vacation. Longtime family friend H.O. Whitney appeared as millionaire H.O. Pittney. He became a central character in Archie's vacation by allowing the boys to stay at his mansion on the lake.

Archie and the gang once again were in New Hampshire for their winter holiday in a series of strips beginning on January 7, 1947, only to return to Riverdale High by the beginning of February. Skiing was the focus of this vacation, with the characters taking a snow train to the Gilford Ski Area. In reality, the ski area was known as the Belknap Mountains Recreation Area in Gilford, and Bob was often seen there looking for inspiration. The Area, as it was called, was home to the first chair lift in the East, and the characters in *Archie* didn't hesitate to take a ride on it when Bob drew it into this series of strips.

The following summer, the characters were back once again on the lake visiting H.O. Pittney. By the winter of 1948, Bob began to include scenes and people from outside the central part of the state. In a series of strips that began on January 8, 1948, Dartmouth College—cleverly renamed Dartboard College—became the feature when Bob sent Veronica and her father there for a class reunion held during the school's annual Winter Carnival. Meredith dentist Dr. Pottle, Hart's Turkey Farm on Ladd Hill and Harry's Garage were some of the lucky early features in the strip.

Bob had masterfully created a world for his characters to live in that included two of his own personal favorites: high school and New Hampshire. He gave the teenagers what he considered the best of both worlds. It didn't take long for residents of Meredith and the Lakes Region to realize what was happening. Suddenly, they had a famous cartoonist circulating among them, and he was getting his inspiration from anything and everything around him. The more he included local scenes and people in the strip, the more the residents understood that they, too, might be drawn into *Archie*. It was an adventure that Bob was taking them on, and they welcomed it with open arms.

Chapter 5

OMIGOSH!

I'm going to settle down here, raise apples and kids, and produce Archie.
—Bob Montana, 1950

Archie's favorite exclamation, "OMIGOSH!" was undoubtedly repeated by residents throughout Meredith when they read the headline in the *Meredith News*, "Cartoonist Plans to Make Meredith His Home." It was the first announcement of the fact that Bob and Peg had decided to become permanent residents:

> *Bob Montana, now a well-known cartoonist and a former resident of Meredith, has returned and is spending the summer at the Herbert C. Knowles camp on Lake Waukewan.*
>
> *Mr. Montana lived here about ten years ago on a farm owned by his father on Meredith Neck. He is the originator of* Archie, *a fairly new comic strip which now appears in forty newspapers throughout the country. Archie's current adventures are based on Meredith and the vicinity. Locations such as Lake Winnipesaukee, Ladd Hill and the railroad station have been reproduced in the comic strip.*
>
> *Bob's father was known in the vaudeville days as "Montana." After vaudeville died, the family moved up here to their farm, which had been their summer home, and opened a restaurant.*
>
> *After 3 and ½ years in the Army, Mr. Montana says that this country is in his blood, and he and his wife are keeping their eyes open for a piece*

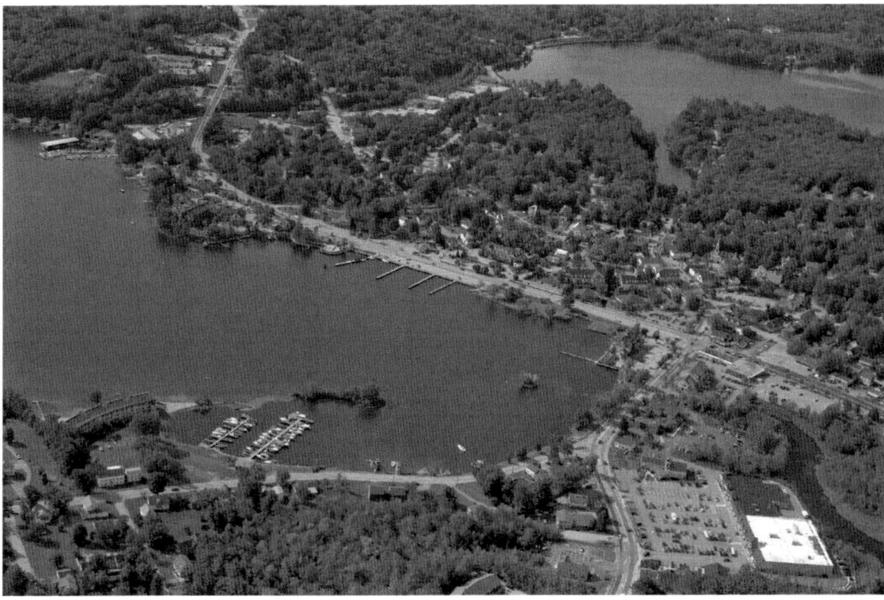

Meredith Bay with Meredith Village (center right) and Lake Waukewan (top right). *Photo by Harrison Haas.*

> *of property where they can build a home. He feels that he can do much better work up here in beautiful surroundings than he can in an apartment in New York City.*[11]

In January 1947, the *Archie* comic strip became a regular weekly feature in the *Meredith News*. The staff of the newspaper was kept busy keeping track of Meredith residents that suddenly appeared in the strip, and each local connection to the comic garnered a front-page announcement. It was the beginning of a lifelong friendship with the staff of the hometown paper and one of many that Bob enjoyed with newspaper editors throughout the state. Editor of the *Meredith News*, Leo Kershaw, and his wife, Ann, became close friends with the entire Montana family.

Bob was becoming as popular as his characters, but he had the ability to take his celebrity status in stride. His fans asked scores of questions, but the most asked was about the source of his humorous ideas. His answer was always the same:

> *I was impressed by Ernest Hemingway's statement that you do your best writing about things you're familiar with. I became familiar with gags and*

> *jokes at an early age. I was born into a vaudeville family and was on the road by the age of three. Growing up backstage, I used to watch and listen from the wings to some of the great humor acts and gagsters of the 1920s.*
>
> *Most of my early schooling was the Calvert courses for professional children taught by my parents and many different grammar schools. After all that, the close relationships, school activities and sports of high school meant a great deal to me. It was a very happy time in my life.*[12]

The *Meredith News* added a new and unique feature to the paper in January 1948. Due to Bob's presence in the community, the weekly paper obtained permission to run six daily *Archie* comic strips in each weekly edition. The paper dropped all other comic strips from its funnies section in favor of running strictly *Archie*. Accompanying the comic strip was the proud by-line: "Archie…By Meredith's Bob Montana."

As the Montanas went about their everyday life, they chose a family doctor and dentist. Dr. Turley, a popular local physician, had the distinction of not only becoming the Montana family physician but also a feature in the *Archie* strip. His appearance caused an impressive front-page write-up in the *Meredith News*. The headline read, "Archie Wins Bout Aided by Dr. Turley":

> *Dr. Raymond J. Turley, popular local physician, was featured from coast to coast this week in the "smash" comic strip* Archie, *produced by Meredith's own Bob Montana. Distributed by McClure's Syndicate, the comic with "Dr. Turley" carefully spelled out on the doctor's bag was released on the 17th for national distribution.*
>
> *Caught with a bad toothache on fight night, Archie is helped by his pal Jughead, who helped himself to a hyperdermic* [sic] *needle filled with Novocain from Dr. Turley's bag. "Enough for three people," says the doctor as he finds the hyperdermic* [sic] *empty.*
>
> *Thus literally feeling "no pain," Archie goes into the fight and is hit with everything but the kitchen sink, but he doesn't even feel it. Then when his opponent has knocked himself out trying his punch on himself to see what the matter is, Archie wins the fight.*[13]

Dr. Frederick Deneault, one of Meredith's most colorful residents, became their dentist. He set up his Meredith practice in 1936 following his graduation from Tufts Dental School and located it in an old, large Victorian on the corner of Main and Waukewan Streets. Little did Dr. Deneault (known as Dr. DeMalt in the strip) ever suspect that he would become a favorite target of the cartoonist. He appeared many times in *Archie*, and even his wife, Dorothea, made a cameo appearance. Bob portrayed Dr. DeMalt as slightly mean and somewhat crazed but offered this explanation for the portrayal: "He's always been my dentist and caused me a lot of pain. This is my way of getting back at him.[14]

Prominent residents and lesser-known places alike were slipped into the comic strip. Archie and Jughead appeared hiking up Red Hill, a nearly two-thousand-foot summit just north of Meredith. Even something as insignificant as the antics of a gray squirrel that caught the attention of Archie and his pals had ties to Meredith. Fans from outside Meredith had no idea that the squirrel appearing in an early strip was actually the pet squirrel of local resident Mary Morgan. The squirrel, known to Mary as His Nibs, was renamed Lootsnoot in the strip.

Having a celebrity living in town fascinated the locals, and organizations couldn't get enough of Bob and his humor. They relentlessly pursued him as a speaker, and most times, despite constant looming deadlines, he gladly accepted invitations. One fall, he had back-to-back engagements, first at the Meredith Rotary Club and then shortly afterward he kept members of the local PTA rolling in the aisles during their first meeting of the school year. As a reporter wrote, "Without trying, he kept the group roaring with laughter with his deft caricatures using local people as models."[15]

The busy schedule Bob maintained was about to get far busier. Peg was expecting their first child. Little Paige Montana was born in the beginning of 1949 and quickly gained the nickname "Paige One," after her rank in the family. Her addition to the family was immortalized soon afterward in the strip when Archie and Jughead were seen sailing in a small boat bearing her name. New grandmother Roberta arrived in Meredith shortly after Paige's birth to stay with the new parents and happily reported that her granddaughter was a "scream."[16]

Bob's personal life was permanently changed by the birth of his first child. His professional life grew in a big way in 1948, the year *Archie* became the number-one selling comic book and in which the comic strip ran in nearly eighty newspapers nationwide. Bob Montana stayed firmly in place as one of America's top cartoonists. That fall, he and twenty-one well-known cartoonists were invited to visit Washington to help get the government's fall bond drive underway. The tour included flying the cartoonists from coast to coast in an aircraft nicknamed the "Flying Cartoonist," which was decorated with the characters created by the cartoonists on board.

When Bob arrived home, Ken Gould, a reporter for the *Meredith News*, caught up with him the day after he returned. Bob explained how he turned out the *Archie* comic strip using Peg (described as a perfect model for either of his glamour girls) as a "laff-meter" to gauge whether or not his ideas for the strip were funny. The reporter mentioned that Meredith residents had been wondering when the newest little Montana was going to make an appearance in her father's comic strip. Bob gave his stock answer: "When she is old enough to sign a release."[17]

The following summer, the Montana family moved into their permanent home on Meredith Neck. The *Meredith News* proudly announced that the Montanas were staying for good:

> *Bob Montana, creator of the comic strip* Archie, *a nationally known comic feature, is to be a year-round resident of here. He has purchased a 16-acre farm that contains a 10-acre apple orchard on the Neck road, which he will make his permanent home.*
>
> *Says Montana, "I'm going to settle down here, raise apples and kids, and produce* Archie.*" Montana knows nothing about the former but has a growing experience on the latter with a daughter and several years of* Archie *production behind him.*
>
> *The farm, which was owned by Skip Sherlock, famous athletic coach from Brookline, Massachusetts, has a large barn in which Montana will make a studio. Its present equipment includes a 3-hole outhouse, which will be retained. "I often get my best ideas while in one," he says.*
>
> *He is undecided on a name for the place, but it will be either Archie Acres or Archie Orchard.*[18]

Their new home consisted of a stately farmhouse and barn perched high upon a hill with impressive views of Lake Winnipesaukee. The original section of the house was built in the 1700s by the Gilman family and had experienced several additions over time. Its dignified appearance and lovely grounds made it one of the most majestic homes in the area.

The excitement over Meredith Neck becoming home to the Montanas was felt throughout the town as well as the Lakes Region. The *Meredith News* took a bow and boasted that its readers were finding great enjoyment in the antics of Archie. Since the addition of the comic strip, subscriptions had increased and nearly 100 percent of the families in Meredith, Sandwich and Moultonborough currently read the paper. It was also noted that word of the great interest of *Archie* had spread far and wide, with more and more

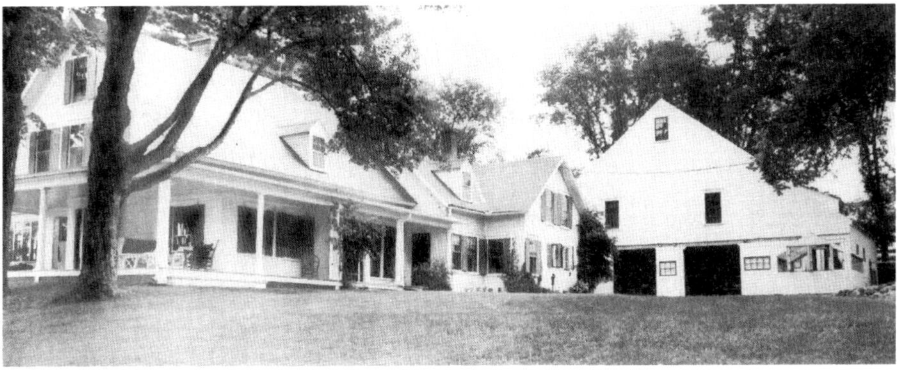

Whitfield Farm, owned by Bob and Peg Montana, included this stately farmhouse situated on a picturesque hilltop. © *Montana family*.

newspapers having joined the ranks of those that ran the strip. Other papers ran an advertising campaign like no other announcing the addition of *Archie* to their lineup of daily comics. However, it was the staff of the *Meredith News* that was the most satisfied. After all, they had been running the comic strip for several years, and the famous creator of *Archie* belonged to Meredith.

Chapter 6

The Love of Family

I am sure that all parents would like to see the time when their youngsters will not want to go to far-off places but love it enough here to stay in Meredith. Let us all try to help them. They are next in line to run our town. They are our future strength both here and in the U.S.A. We need them.

—Roberta Montana, March 1953

Bob Montana's parents naturally instilled a love of family in both Ruth and him. Raymond and Roberta had always been attentive to their children and possessed an intense interest in their activities. When Bob and Peg purchased their farmhouse, Roberta moved to Meredith permanently in order to be closer to her son and his growing family. The Montanas were a close-knit family, but they had a definite knack for making friends feel like they were a welcome part of it.

Just as Bob and Peg were settling into their new house, cartoonist Dick Brooks arrived in town with his wife and daughter and chose to rent a cottage down the road from the Montanas' home. The cartoonists planned on working together, as Dick had been hired as Bob's assistant. Dick was already familiar with *Archie* since he worked for Bob while the Montanas wintered during previous years in Westport, Connecticut. In addition, Dick was working on his own comic strip named the *Jackson Twins*, and he was fortunate to be able to learn comic-strip techniques from a true master.

Whitfield Farm had been chosen as the official name of the Montana homestead—Whitfield being a name from Peg's side of the family. However, to local residents and visiting friends, the lovely farmhouse and the land surrounding it was affectionately known as the Montana Compound. With Peg's elegant touches to domestic life and Bob's interest and abilities in farming, their home and gardens flourished.

Bob still possessed a love for the lake, and in the spring of 1951, he became the third owner of an almost forty-year-old, twenty-eight-foot Friendship sloop named the *White Eagle*. Like its new owner, the vessel enjoyed its own fame, as it had appeared in the movie *Carousel*. Bob's sloop was built in Friendship, Maine, by Wilbur Morse, who had gained a reputation for constructing quality sloops that were considered high-performance vessels. The elegant yet practical craft was transported by trailer from Boothbay Harbor in Maine and subsequently launched at Channel Marine in the Weirs, a small section of Laconia. The Montanas planned to repaint the sloop, complete minor repairs themselves and have her ready to sail by mid-May.

The sloop was docked in Gilford with the Winnipesaukee Yacht Club, a popular sailing club founded in 1937. Every Sunday during the summer,

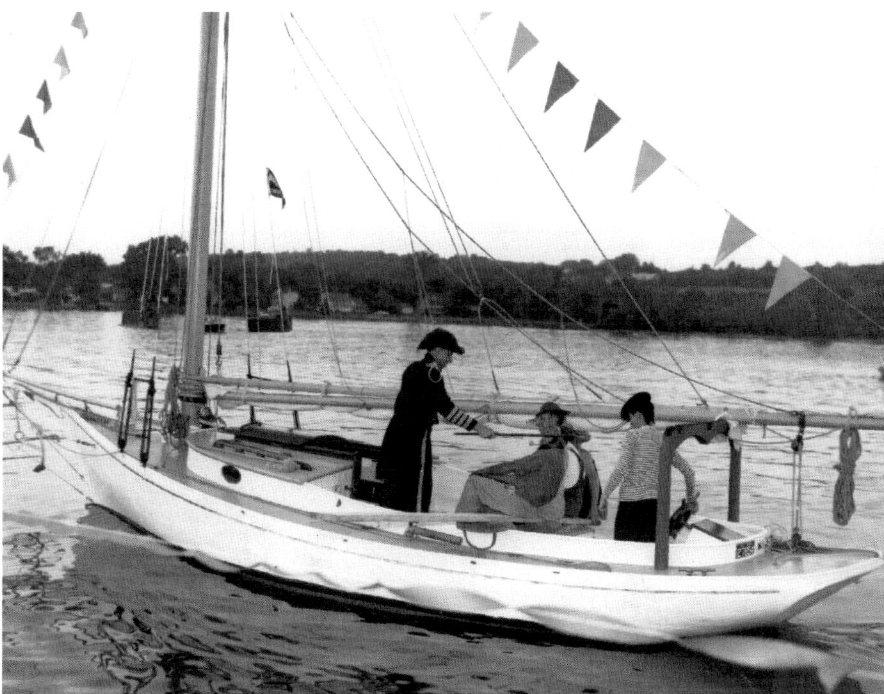

Bob's Friendship sloop, the *White Eagle*, sailing the waters of Lake Winnipesaukee. *Courtesy of Meredith Historical Society*.

club members sponsored and competed in sailing races on the lake and at other locations throughout the region.[19] Bob and Peg became members of the club and were active in the organization's entertainment committee. It didn't take long for a boat name the *Eagle* to appear in *Archie*, and Bob snuck the yacht club into the strip, calling it the Winnabanana Yacht Club.

The *White Eagle* wasn't the only addition to the Montana family that year. In the fall, Bob and Peg welcomed their second daughter, Lynn, into the world. Bob was living up to his statement that he planned on raising apples and kids and producing *Archie*. That fall, the apple harvest was abundant, he was the father of two children and his professional life was blossoming beyond his expectations.

Shortly after the arrival of Lynn, Bob left on an air tour with eighteen other cartoonists. The U.S. Air Force, using two C-47 planes, flew the men nearly eight thousand air miles in seven days while showing them their latest equipment and methods. The round-trip tour began and ended in Washington, D.C., with stops at various air force bases across the country. Before embarking on the trip, each cartoonist was invited to create a drawing featuring their main characters participating in a presidential breakfast. The drawings were impressive, but it was Bob's that *Life* magazine gave top billing in its December 3, 1951 edition.

Back home in Meredith, headlines announced the appearance of the drawing in *Life*, and local retailers were nowhere near prepared for the onslaught of *Archie* fans rushing through their doors to purchase a copy. The edition was an immediate sell-out in Meredith and surrounding towns, but the magazine gladly arranged for a special distribution of the issue throughout the Lakes Region. The original drawing never made it back to Meredith. It was retained for inclusion in a permanent display at the Truman Museum, which was in the process of being built in Independence, Missouri.

There was no stopping the popularity explosion of the *Archie* comic strip. In January 1952, Archie's fame had spread to Europe, as it had finally broken into the European market when it was published in the Stockholm *Europa Press*. Prior to this breakthrough, the strip appeared outside the United States in Canadian and Mexican newspapers. *Archie* had become truly international.

Millions of fans throughout the world saw the people and places of New Hampshire. That spring, Bob decided to include Meredith's Key Theatre in *Archie*, which captured the attention of local residents. It was one of several times he featured it. The next time the theatre was visited by Archie, Bob drew his mother in as the cashier, one of the rare times a family member

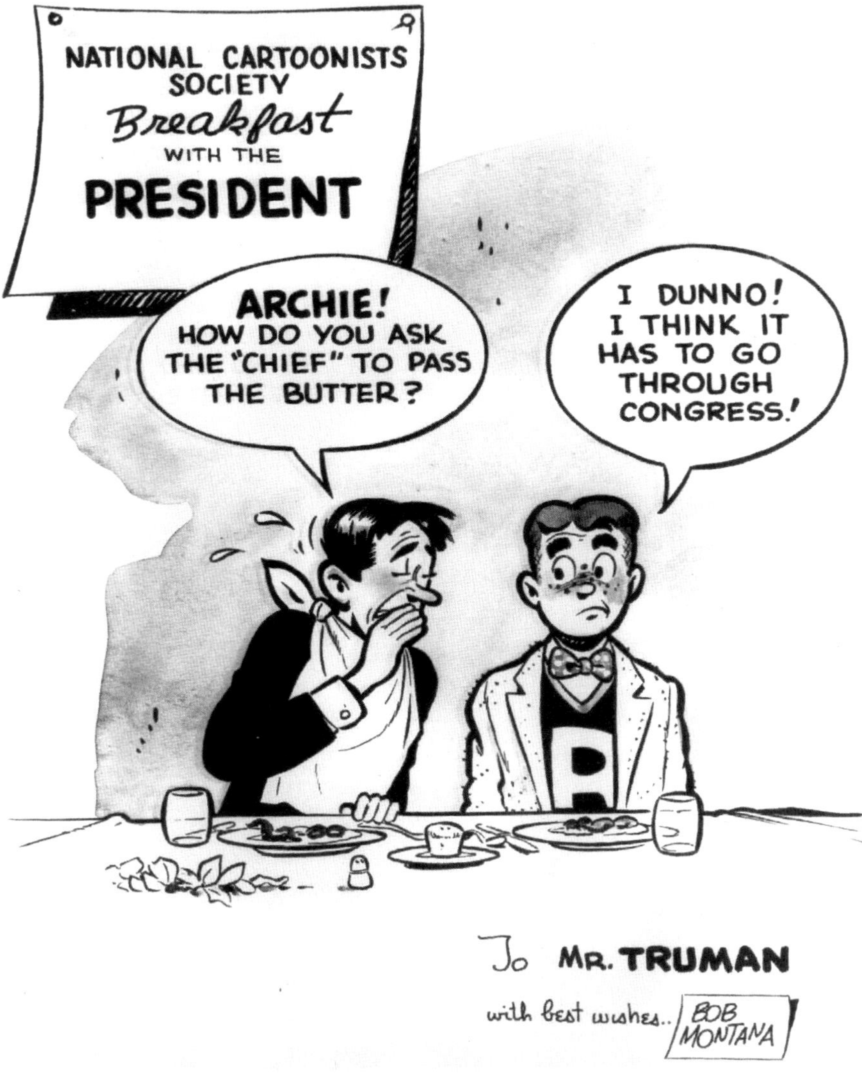

Life magazine gave this presidential breakfast *Archie* comic top billing in its December 1951 edition. © *Montana family*.

made an appearance. Locals had no trouble recognizing the establishment or Roberta Montana. She, too, had become a well-known and celebrated member of the Meredith community.

Bob was known throughout the world, yet he remained grounded and unchanged. His family and life in Meredith were his focus; community news

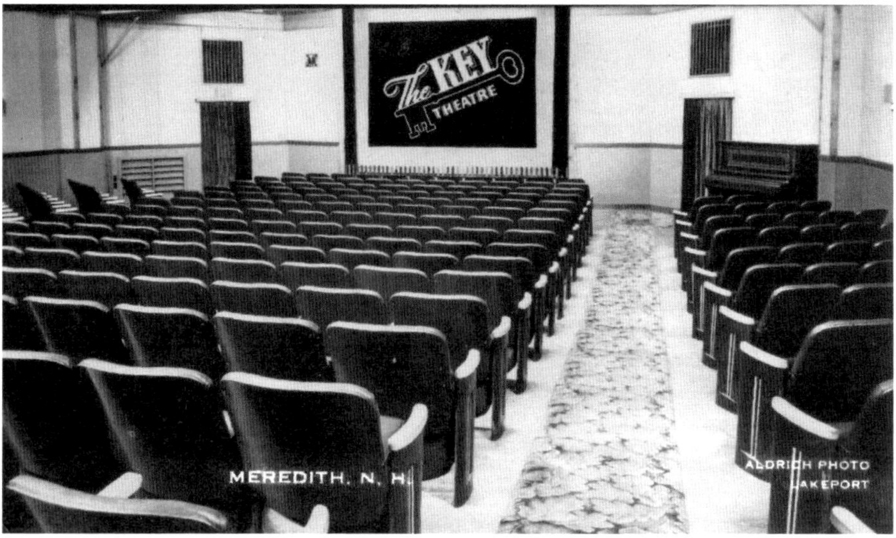

The Key Theatre, a popular Meredith attraction, was often visited by Archie and his pals in the comic strip. *Courtesy of Meredith Historical Society.*

and events captured his attention. It was the same for Roberta, who was busy running a dance studio that she had opened on Main Street.

In March 1953, the principal discussion in town concerned the need for a gym to be used by its growing number of young people. At a school meeting where the topic was to be discussed, it was barely mentioned. Roberta, who had been looking forward to the discussion, immediately wrote a letter to the editor of the *Meredith News*, explaining her disappointment that the subject had been disrespectfully ignored. She included her thoughts on what she felt adults should be doing for the next generation: "In the first place, anything that makes for the happiness and healthfulness of our next generation is important. We must give them happy memories of Meredith so that they will want to remain here and want to come back here. We must show them we want them by showing them we are considering their welfare."[20]

When residents attended yet another meeting held specifically to discuss and then vote on the expenditure for the gym, reporters were there in force. Later, a story ran that described Bob's influence on the outcome of the vote:

> *Robert "Bob" Montana, creator of the internationally popular comic strip* Archie, *again gave indication of the respect of his judgment by the citizens of his home, Meredith, New Hampshire, recently at the district school meeting there. Faced with a large expenditure, the community, already*

> *straining its finances, had noted for the basic school and appropriated funds for it.*
>
> *Then came the question, should the gymnasium-auditorium, at a cost of $210,000, be included? Sentiment was running strongly against the added expense, although it was generally admitted the need was great. The only speaker from the floor in favor of the construction of the addition was Bob. With a few well-chosen remarks, he impressed on the large gathering the necessity of including the gymnasium-auditorium in the project. When the vote was taken a few minutes later, the result was an overwhelmingly 12 to 1 ratio vote for the complete building.*[21]

Roberta was not the only one who would stand up for the young people in Meredith. Bob learned early on that his celebrity status could be used for the betterment of his community, and he could make great strides where others struggled or failed. Like mother, like son; Roberta found her own way to help the young people of Meredith. After the vote, she opened the doors of her dance studio to local teenagers once a week in the evening and offered them an opportunity to gather there for a dance, music and refreshments. She promised to host the event once a week until the new gym was built.

The Montanas' full-time residency and their involvement in community affairs had a definite effect on the *Archie* comic strip. No longer was it front-page news when something native appeared in the strip. The *Meredith News* simply could not keep up with the number of appearances. Instead, it became a guessing game for residents, and they loved it. Bob had such a great talent for drawing caricatures that he could include a local and then let readers figure out the individual's identity.

When town residents began to appear at Riverdale High, the line between the two worlds had become blurred. Local schoolgirl Leah Knowles became Meredith High School's Miss Cheerleader in 1951. That February, she appeared in the strip as a Carnival Queen contestant at Riverdale High. Archie and his pals visited the Lakes Region throughout the year, not just during school vacations. One thing was for certain: when they arrived, mayhem was guaranteed.

Bob would often include the name of a business or individual as is or only slightly changed. In January 1951, Bacon's Self-Service Laundry appeared in the strip with the same name. Parissi's Italian Restaurant retained its name as well. However, Sprague's Service Station on Main Street turned into Sprig's. The name of True's Gift Shop appeared on the store window when it appeared in *Archie*, but the name of the store clerk was omitted. However,

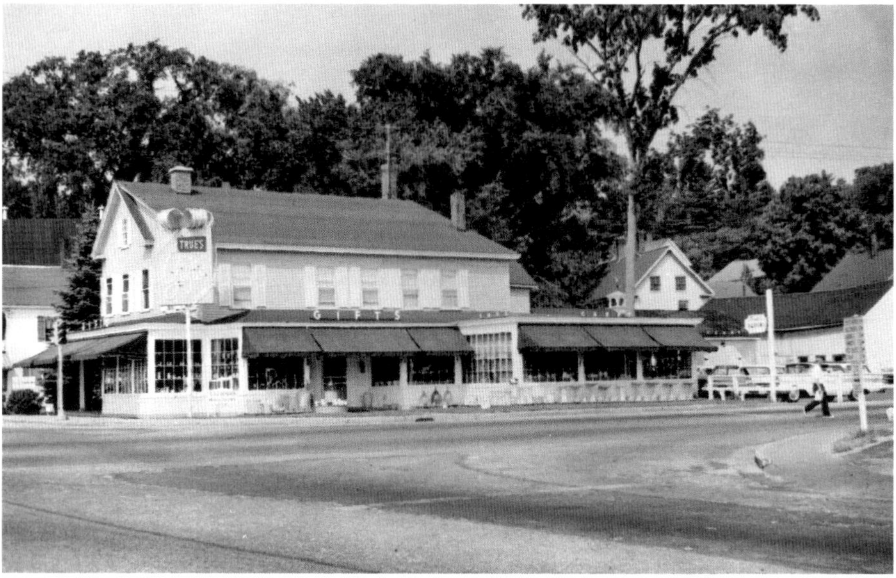

True's Gift Shop was featured several times in *Archie*. *Courtesy of Meredith Historical Society.*

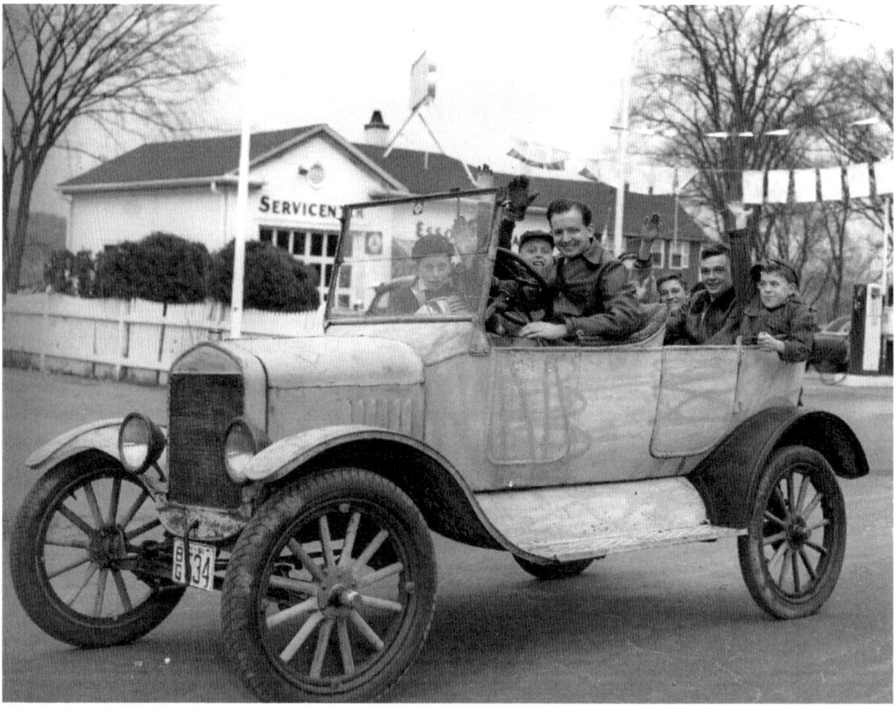

Bob would often pack his Model-T Ford with local youngsters and take them for a spin around the town. © *Montana family*.

she was easily identifiable to those who knew her, proven by a letter received by the *Meredith News* from a reader living in New Haven, Connecticut, who stated that she had no trouble identifying the store clerk.

Scenes from all over the state were drawn into the strip during the appropriate seasons. During the winter of 1951, Veronica skied at Ragged Mountain, a New Hampshire ski area, and Archie wrangled with a classic old rope tow. During the warmer months, Archie was a contestant in a car race up Mount Washington, the highest peak in the White Mountains and a summit known for its extreme weather. A sign pointed the way to Tuckerman Ravine, which is, in reality, located on the east side of the mountain. On the trip back down, the Mount Washington Cog Railway, a National Historic Engineering Landmark, was utilized by the teenage competitors.

The *Archie* comic strip had become Bob's adult diary. During the Mount Washington auto race, Archie used his Model T Ford. Bob could have done the same since he, too, owned a Model T. In comparing Archie's life to Bob's, it is difficult to tell whose life was the busiest. The pace of Bob's life was hectic, but he was enjoying himself. Life was good for the entire Montana family, and even though it seemed as if it couldn't get busier or better, it most certainly did both.

Chapter 7

Meredith Village Players

Playing to packed houses for three nights, Mutiny on the Mount, *Bob Montana's prize-winning musical comedy, scored an all-time high rating for local productions. From the opening lines of the prologue to the final curtain, this fast-stepping musical show moved rapidly from one hilarious situation to another.*
—Meredith News, *June 26, 1952*

Late in 1949, a talented group of thespians came together in Meredith to showcase their acting skills by putting on a play for the local women's club. Although it was intended to be a casual, amateur production, the show was a resounding hit. So gratifying was the experience for the actors that they decided to continue with more theatrical productions, and the drama club known as the Meredith Village Players was born.

Small, short plays were produced throughout the winter. In mid-April 1950, their production *Hometown Minstrels* was shown for three nights, with large audiences cramming into the town hall each evening. Witnessing the intense interest in the play, the American Legion offered the Players the use of its hall for one night per month.

By the end of April, over thirty individuals banded together to formalize the organization. They held their first meeting at the home of Gwen Flather and her husband, Ralph, a respected architect in the Lakes Region. A board of directors was formed, and those in attendance were well-known names around town: Bacon, Bucklin, Grad, Miner, Montana, Plummer, Roper and Turley. Meredith's popular song leader and dentist, Doc Pottle, was part of

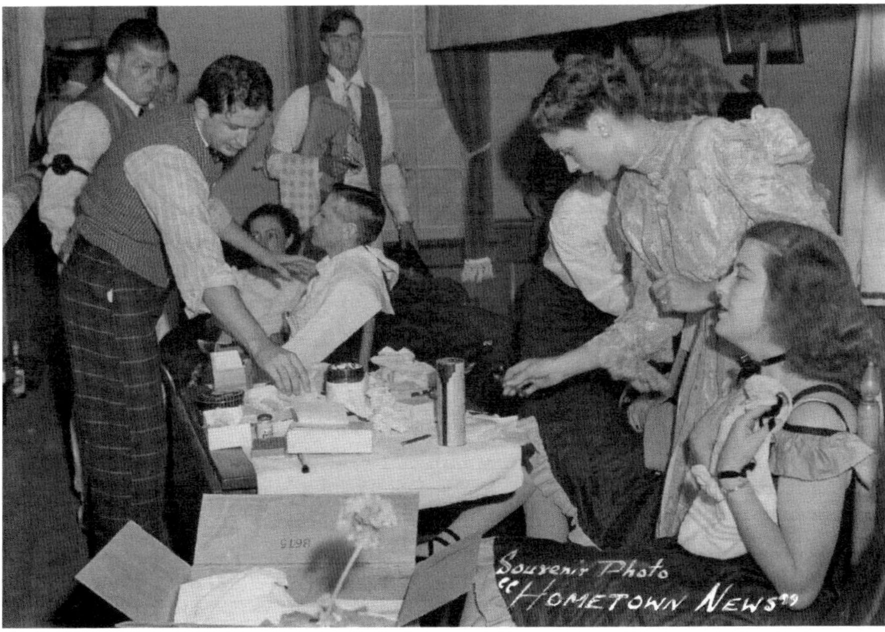

Backstage during a show, Bob (second from left) applies makeup as Peg (second from right) assists. *Courtesy of Meredith Historical Society.*

the assembly of gifted individuals. With the constitution and by-laws written, members of the newly formed organization were energized and set out to recruit more members to work on their first big production.

Summer turned into fall, and handfuls of members were planning, choosing cast members, designing scenery and rehearsing at least two times a week. In October, the Players came out swinging with their first public production, *The Real McCoy*. Gwen Flather had been chosen as director since she had extensive experience as a member of the Players in Newton, Massachusetts, and the Boston Stage Society. Ruth Beede was in charge of designing the scenery and had previously worked on stage sets for Gilford's Gaslight Players, the Winnipesaukee Ski Club and the Winnipesaukee Yacht Club.

The Montanas had been working behind the scenes. Bob and Peg hung numerous hand-painted posters around town to advertise the play. Not many of the Players' productions went forward without the skillful application of stage makeup by none other than the ex-Ziegfeld dancer and vaudeville performer Roberta Montana. Even Archie got swept up in the excitement when he took Veronica to see *The Real McCoy* in the comic strip.

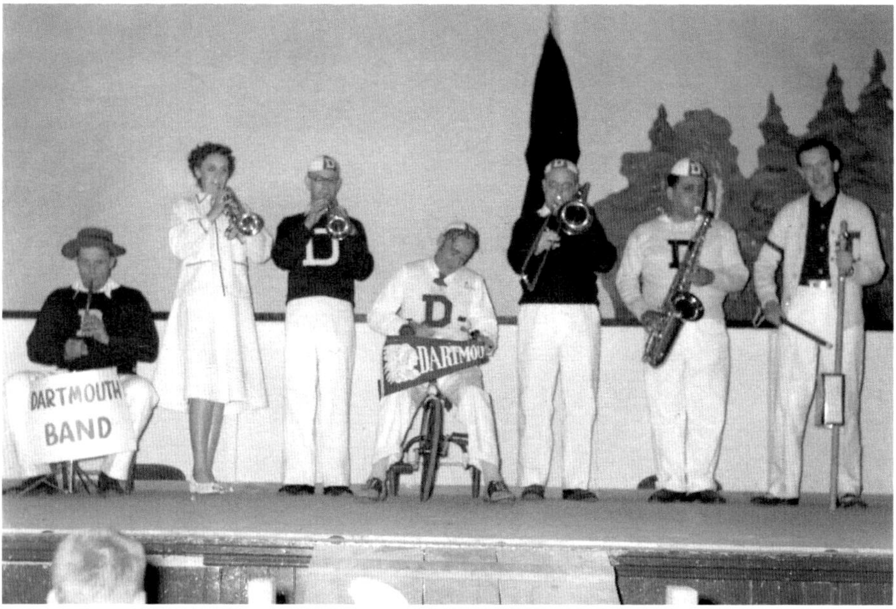

Never without his famous Jazzstick, Bob (far right) plays it during a production of the Meredith Village Players. *Courtesy of Meredith Historical Society.*

Audiences were in for a treat. Not only did the Players put on a fantastic production, but the play also included something that many had not witnessed. Bob Montana was slated to play his Jazzstick, an instrument that dated back to the time the Montana family owned their restaurant in town.

The Jazzstick was Bob's boyhood creation that caused two pieces of Roberta's cleaning items to fall prey to her inventive son. Her broom, with its wooden handle, became the main piece of the instrument. Eight nails, each with four bottle caps attached, were hammered into the handle here and there up to within five or six inches of the top. The bottom was put through an oblong gallon oilcan. The accompanying drumstick was made from the handle of Roberta's doomed mop, with notches added along it for approximately one foot. A rhythm could be created by running the notches of the drumstick along the broom handle, which jingled the bottle caps. The oilcan and the broom handle were used to create a drum sound. From the time the homemade instrument was created, it was always within Bob's reach, and it traveled with him throughout the world.[22]

The Real McCoy, featuring Bob and his Jazzstick, played to packed houses and was declared an overwhelming success. The theatrical group immediately gained the reputation as being professional and top-notch. The public made it clear that it wanted more, and the group graciously offered productions throughout the following year.

Return Engagement was the Players' spring 1951 show. This time, Roberta was a cast member in the play, and Bob handled the makeup. The following February, the Players were ready to perform an adaptation of the Russian farce *Chords and Dischord*. With Roberta acting as director of the one-act play, it was successful and well attended.

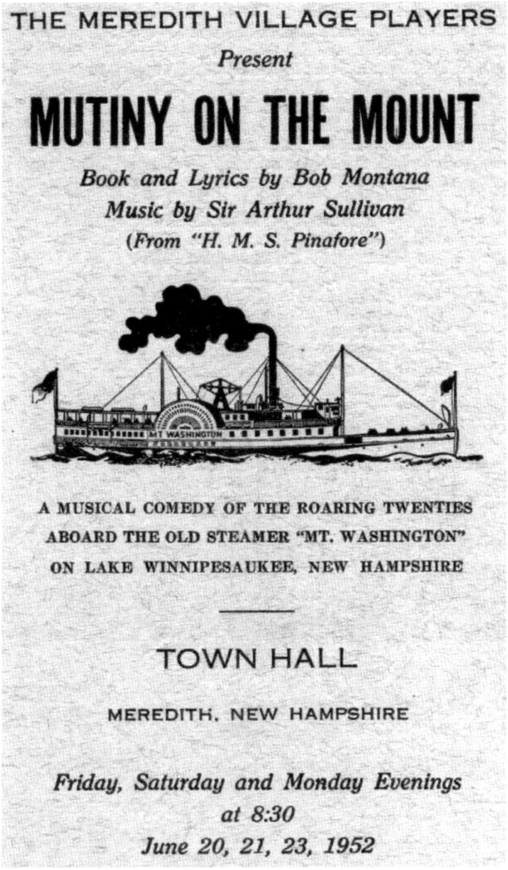

Program cover for the award-winning *Mutiny on the Mount*, a play written by Bob for the Meredith Village Players. *Courtesy of Meredith Historical Society*.

The Players continued to blast through previous boundaries. Members were challenged by a contest to find the best playwright in the organization. In the spring of 1952, the first fifty-dollar playwright prize went to Bob Montana for the play he wrote in his spare time. The group then moved forward with plans to present it to the public. Called *Mutiny on the Mount*, it was a comedy set halfway through the glorious Roaring Twenties aboard the infamous steamship *Mount Washington*.[23]

Shortly after picking Bob's play as the winner, the Players chose members for the production staff of the comedy. Complications arose when they set the presentation date for the first week of June, as Bob had been scheduled for an overseas USO trip to the European theater. Fortunately, the trip was postponed by the army until midsummer, giving the Players ample time to fine-tune and present their play.

The production reached new heights. The scenery and costume guilds stopped at nothing to make every detail of the drama as realistic as possible.

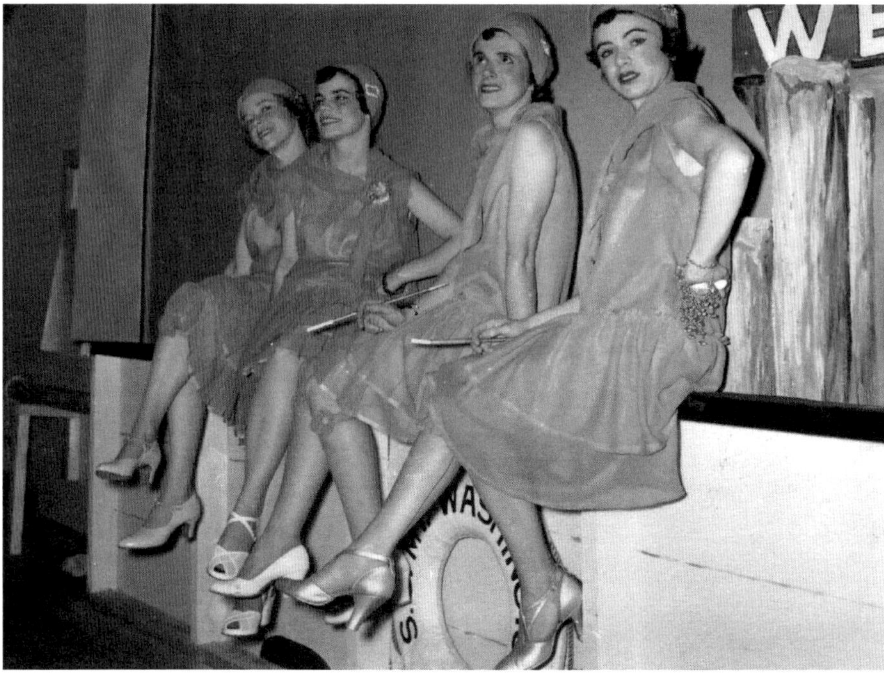

Meredith Village Players actresses. *From left to right*: Annalee Thorndike, Sue Valliere, Ruth Harding and June Allen. *Courtesy of Meredith Historical Society.*

The deck of the old steamship was reproduced, and the costumes were given a high rating, with flapper and Joe College–era clothing out in the forefront. A collegiate band offered musical entertainment on the boat, two pianists played from the wings and Bob was there to entertain with his Jazzstick. The cast included many notable actresses, such as Annalee Thorndike, creator of the Meredith-based and world-famous Annalee Dolls. Bob's assistant, Ruth Harding, jumped at the chance to become a cast member. When not acting, she worked closely with Bob, inked the strips and offered comical ideas that he could expand on and include in *Archie*.

It came as no surprise that hoards of summer residents had reserved seats, many out-of-town people were in attendance and celebrities from Boston and New York were seen among the audience. The fame of the Meredith Village Players had spread far and wide.

After the play ran the course of three nights of performances, a *Meredith News* headline read "Meredith Village Players Score Again: Bob Montana's Mutiny on the Mount a Hilarious Hit—Plays to Packed Houses." The article described the characters and the complexity of the play:

Lloyd Bigelow, known to patrons of the Meredith Trust Co. as a genial teller, was a totally different person in the role of the frustrated naval hero Captain Snarlson of the old side-wheeler "Mt. Washington."

Syne Batchelder, one of the proprietors of Martin and Batchelder's and a member of Meredith's School Board, depicted a naïve, hillbilly sailor who told in song of his domestic troubles in his shack in Holderness and how he came to "seek employ and take a job as a sailor boy," along with Dick Guion and "Chick" Harding, who also were sailors.

Bob Rhodes, Meredith's town manager, forgot his troubles when he assumed the role of a college boy with his pals Al Aucoin (local High School teacher), Larry Sage (Keasbey and Mattison) and Al Quirk (Quirk's Electric Shop). Shel Miner, known in the Lakes Region as an able accountant, used his ukulele to attract the flappers of 1925. He also gave Henry Ogglebee (Guy Horne, Town Clerk and Insurance), one of the Judges in the Beauty Contest, advice on how to make time with the girls. Mildred, Ogglebee's domineering wife, was played by Dorothy Nedeau, known throughout the state as president of the Association of Farm Women.

Included in the cast were the bathing beauties of 1952: Florence Rice as Miss Center Harbor; Jean Guion, Miss Moultonborough; Jane Flather, Miss Weirs; Peggy Montana, Miss Wolfeboro; and Ada Batchelder, Miss Meredith.[24]

After the resounding success of its major production that year, the group wanted to show its appreciation for the community's support and gave a free performance in December as a gift to the town. Nearly four hundred people packed into the town hall to watch the production.

The 1953 summer production of the Village Players was a three-act comedy called *Caleb's Folly*, written by Ralph Flather and skillfully directed by his wife, Gwen. Set in New Hampshire and Mexico during 1910, the cast of almost fifty-four members kept the comedy fast-paced and spirited.

The syndicated play *Miranda* became the Players' production of choice for the summer of 1954. June Allen snatched the starring role as Miranda, while John Jewett stepped into the role of director. A new member of the group, John had arrived in Meredith one year prior and had vast experience in directing theatricals. Again, the newspaper provided a report:

All roads will lead to the Town Hall on Thursday, Friday and Saturday evenings of this week in June, when each year those who enjoy a good play always look forward to a fine production from the Meredith Village Players.

> *This year, they are presenting the Broadway comedy hit "Miranda," with a dress rehearsal last Tuesday night, when director John Jewett gave final instructions to the cast and "Dooley" Weeks was on hand with his camera.*
>
> *The leading lady of this year's production will be June Allen as Miranda, whose mysterious attractions prove alluring to all the men and upsetting to the ladies of the play. Chet Lord will be adequate as the philandering doctor Sir Paul Marten, who brings Miranda into his house as a guest to the dismay of Lady Marten, played by Virginia Graf. Lady Marten's chum Isabel, who is the proprietress of a swank hat shop, will be a congenial role for Isabel Russell, who has appeared in many of the Players' productions. Dick Aieta plays opposite Isabel as a cosmopolitan man-about-town with artistic tastes.*[25]

The Players performed in front of enthralled audiences. To celebrate the group's continuing success, the Montanas hosted a summer picnic at their farm for over sixty-five people. Bob ran a circus booth for the kids, with Chick Harding handing out lemonade and popcorn. The children were further entertained with pony rides and a ride in one of Bob's most beloved possessions, his red Model T Ford (a spin in it was enjoyed by some of the adults as well).

The picnic held a few surprises, and one was the presentation of a newly created Players' Outstanding Performance Award, or the POP. That year, the gold-plated, engraved trophy was given to June Allen for her outstanding performance as Miranda. With the award being the organization's version of the theatrical Oscar, there was plenty of competition, and the candidates were required to go through two panels of judges.

Chairman Bunce Bacon announced after the picnic that the group's goal was to present a major production that fall in addition to the annual spring play. After the presentations and announcements, the picnic finished off with a spur-of-the-moment show that began with a drawing contest between Bob Montana and Tom Graf.

A fall production never transpired. Instead, the Players switched gears and became involved with moviemaking, one of Bob's favorite hobbies. In the spring of 1955, the Village Players presented what they called their world-premiere movie, *The Deed*. A silent western, it was written and produced by members of the Players, and those appearing in the film experienced their first cinematic roles. Chick Harding starred as the Powder River Kid, Bunce Bacon as Breezy and Dick Guion as Jack Diamond. Ruth Harding created the costumes, and Roberta returned to makeup.

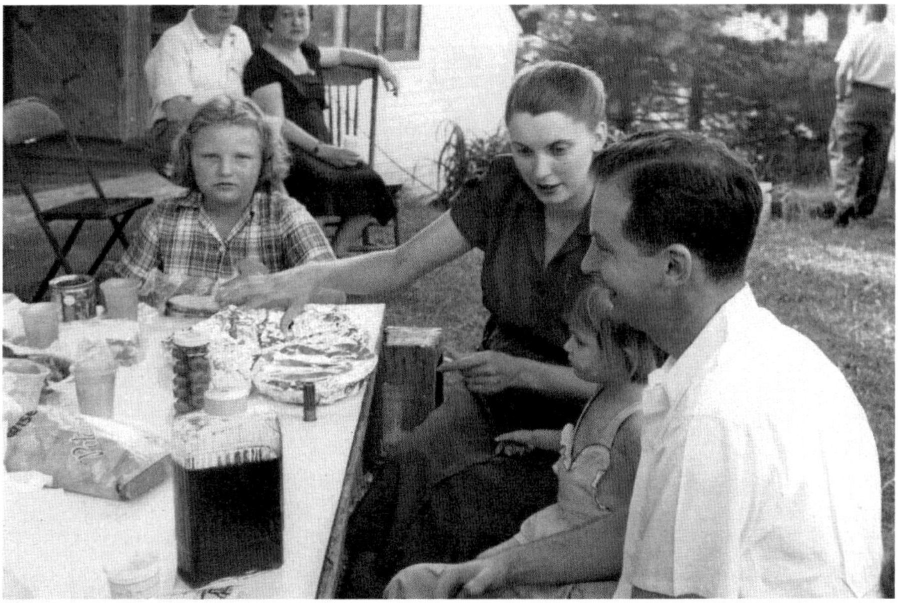

Bob and Peg Montana often hosted picnics for the Meredith Village Players at Whitfield Farm. *Courtesy of Meredith Historical Society.*

Bob directed the eight-millimeter film on a set that had been built on the Montana farm. He experimented with his own moviemaking aptitude, as well as the Players' abilities to become film stars. The premiere of the pilot caused quite a sensation in town, which confirmed what Bob already knew: the Village Players were ready for the movies. His creative mind had skipped ahead and was hard at work on the development of the script for their next film.

Chapter 8

The Close Shave

This year, the production will be a 45-minute old-time movie entitled The Close Shave. *Janet Grad, chairman of the Players, says that this is one of the most ambitious projects the Players have ever undertaken.*
—Meredith News, *February 1956*

The fascinating brainchild of Bob Montana, a movie called *The Close Shave*, was undoubtedly a highly ambitious, challenging and exotic project. Although the Meredith Village Players had already produced a movie, this film tested the skills of all those involved in its creation. One would expect Bob to create a humorous movie; however, the story behind the name he gave the film is far from comical. Its origin is connected to a frightening incident that occurred almost thirty years prior.

On January 12, 1927, Raymond and Roberta Montana, along with Bobby and Ruth, were traveling by train through New York. They were suddenly thrust into the middle of an attempted train robbery when one of the two criminals involved held a revolver to Roberta's head. The following day, she wrote a letter to the editor of the *Meredith News* to let their friends in Meredith know they had not been harmed. In her letter, she described every detail of the frightening crime:

> *An experience which few of us ever have and many of us hope to never have was the lot of the Montana family last night. Montana the Cowboy Banjoist, who is playing the Keith Albee Vaudeville Circuit, always carries*

his wife and two children with him wherever he goes. Last night, they were aboard the Keystone Express going from Johnston, New York, to East Liberty. As is the case with most performers, Montana and the two kiddies, Ruth and Bobby, settled themselves for a little nap, leaving me to interest myself in a book, and now I will write you what happened.

I was deeply interested in my storybook when I experienced the feeling that someone was standing quite near me. Lifting my eyes slowly from the book I was reading, I looked squarely into an automatic 38, and you may be sure that there and then I lost all interest in my reading. From the muzzle of the gun, which stood about 10 or 12 inches from my face, I lifted my eyes to the person above it, and there I found a horribly bloated and distorted set of features.

My first thought was to bluff him off, but as his hand which held the gun shook horribly, I could only think of how I could make him point that most threatening muzzle away from me without scaring or angering him.

Very carefully, I pushed Mr. Montana with my toe (he was sitting opposite me), making sure my move should not be seen...then something made me speak, and in a cool clear voice I said, "Please have a little pity for the two kiddies" (the magic word), for instantly he looked at them and said, "AH, I'm sorry lady," and moved on down the isle [sic] *to hold up two men at the farther end of the car, also the conductor and brakeman.*[26]

The criminals were apprehended after being tackled by a brakeman on the station platform when they tried to flee. The Montanas were shaken but unharmed, and from then on, the family always referred to that incident as their "close shave."

Bob must have had the name of that childhood incident in the back of his mind when he picked a title for the Players' movie. In February 1956, he hosted screen tests for all actors that were willing to accept the challenge of becoming local silver screen stars and starlets. The goal of the group was to have the film completed in time to present it to the community as their annual spring production.

The Montanas hosted the organization's next meeting at their homestead, and members were able to view themselves as film stars when Bob rolled the footage of the auditions. John Jewett agreed to direct the movie, the cast was chosen and a schedule of dates for filming was set. The *Meredith News* was already advertising the project, stating in an article, "One will be watching for the rolling eyes, the dancing hips and the many other interesting incidents of this movie."[27]

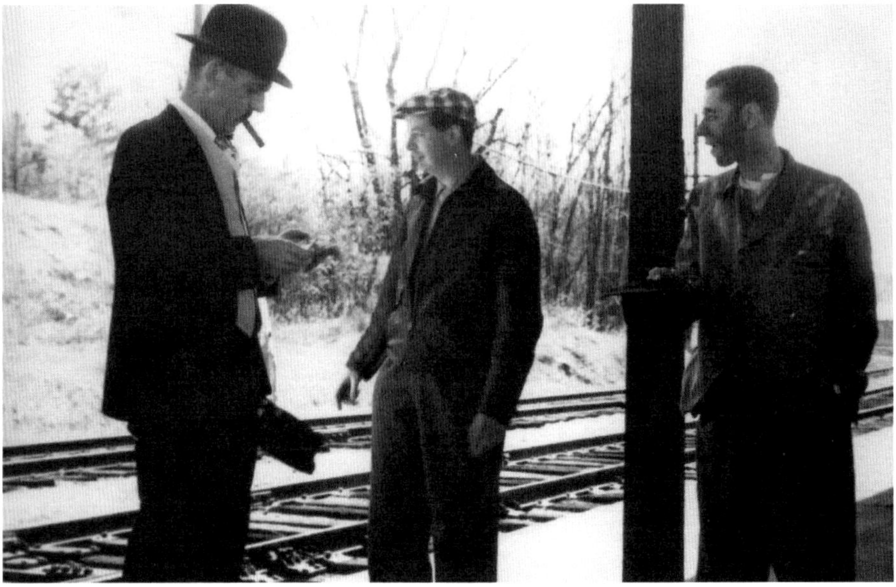

Bob (center) directs Dick Guion (left) and Will Grad during the filming of *The Close Shave*. *Courtesy of Meredith Historical Society.*

Filming began on the first Sunday in April and continued every Sunday thereafter until the taping was finished. Coordination of the actors and actresses did not compare to the coordination and cooperation required from the various town departments. The police department shut down certain streets in Meredith during filming, the fire station was used during one scene, numerous businesses turned into movie sets and even the Boston & Maine Railroad donated the use of a train for the opening scene.

What resulted was a thirty-five-minute film that reaches far beyond the amateur category, and the finished product shows Bob's artful mastery of filmmaking. The silent black-and-white film is entertaining, comical and intriguing, yet it is also one of the best historical documentations of Meredith during the 1950s. Some locals were cast as fictional characters; others played themselves. Prominent landmarks and town residents can be spotted throughout the action-packed saga; sadly, many are no longer with us.

As the film begins, the stage is set. The year is 1925, "when the Roaring Twenties were just a growl," as the movie's headline reads. Will Grad, of the family-run store Grad's, turns in a riveting performance in his role as Harold Smelt, a likeable yet typical hobo. He rolls into town aboard a steaming locomotive, and the action begins at the train station. His stroll down Main

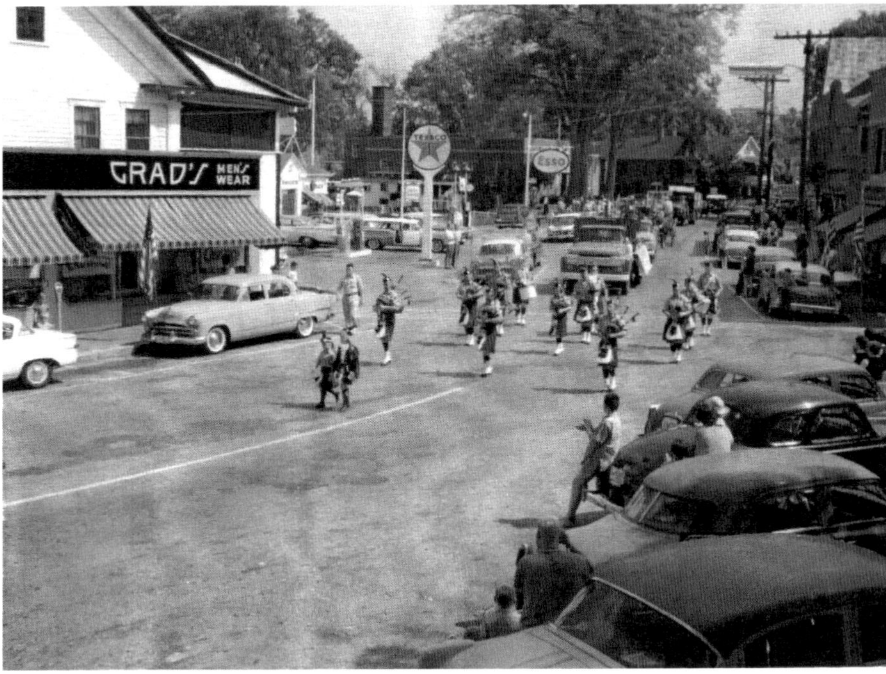

Family owned and operated Grad's on Main Street. *Courtesy of Meredith Historical Society.*

Street not only gets him into trouble but also highlights familiar sights: Pynn's Garage, the Humiston School, Meredith Public Library, the in-town canal and the Allen Barber Shop.

Shortly afterward, Smelt meets the lovely Violet Noggincropper and her father, Pop Noggincropper, the local barber, played by Stella Roux and Adam Kehl, respectively. The plot thickens as it unfolds into a classic boy-loves-loses-and-wins-the-girl storyline. Viewers are taken on a trip through Meredith, beginning with the Meredith Diner as the finagling hobo stops in for a bite to eat.

After a quick stop at the local barbershop for a shave, Harold is transformed into a respectable-looking citizen. His visit there pushes him into a career as a barber, and almost simultaneously, he begins competing with the movie's villain for the affections of the head-turning Violet. Twists and turns in the plot include a spirited fencing match between the two suitors, while two thugs, Dirty Dick and Ray the Rat, frame the unsuspecting Harold for a bank robbery at the Meredith Village Savings Bank. Despite all the challenges and battles, the movie concludes with an optimistic ending, as Violet happily becomes Mrs. Harold Smelt. The newlyweds' departure from town causes the local barber

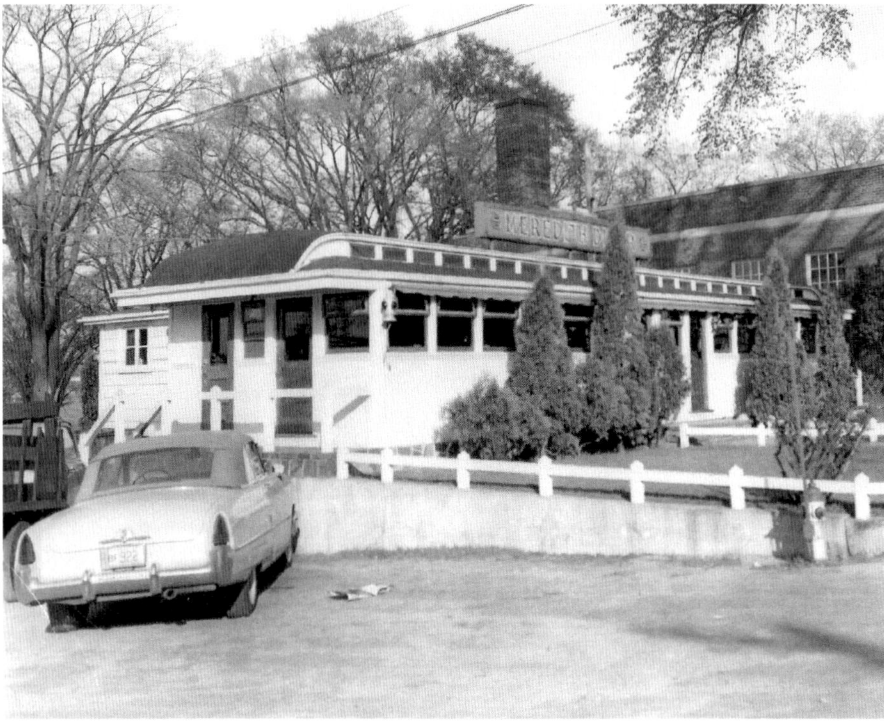

The Meredith Diner, formerly a predominant landmark located next to the post office, was spotlighted in *The Close Shave*. *Courtesy of Meredith Historical Society*.

to once again place a help-wanted sign in the front window of his shop. Jesse Allen, Meredith's legendary barber, gets the last laugh in the final scene of the movie, as he is shown entering the shop to apply for the position. It was Jesse's Main Street barbershop that was used during the filming.

The public's reception of the Players' premiere movie was astounding. The popular movie was played at numerous showings and continued to be shown in the years that followed. As the dust settled after the movie's dazzling debut, the Village Players held their annual awards program at the end of June. Will Grad was honored with the Players' annual POP Award for his impressive portrayal of Harold Smelt. Bob Montana received the Author's Award for his creation and production of the film.

Filmmaking was an art form that Bob had a yearning to master. It fascinated him from the time he first saw talking pictures during his vaudeville days, and after producing *The Close Shave*, he knew that he could produce a quality film. This was all part of his constant desire to better himself—to try something different—and in doing so, he inspired others to do the same.

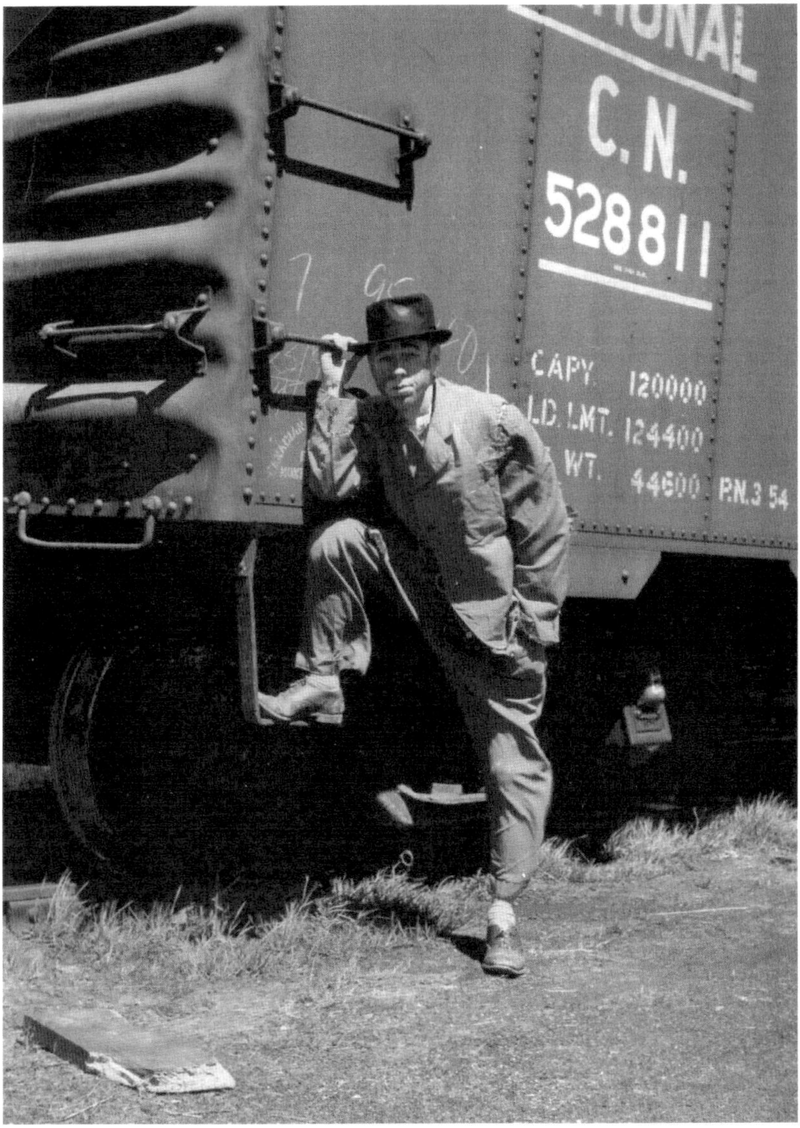

Willard Grad as the hobo, Harold Smelt, in *The Close Shave. Courtesy of Meredith Historical Society.*

The production of this movie coincided with the final curtain dropping on the fast-paced activities and widely acclaimed productions of the Meredith Village Players. In general, people were less inclined to set aside time for socializing in groups, which triggered a shift in society and its structure. At the time *The Close Shave* was being created, Meredith's Key Theatre closed its doors. Owner Joe Kennedy blamed the advent and popularity of television for the low number of individuals watching movies anywhere except in the comfort of their own living rooms. He made one last attempt to keep the theater open only on weekends. It continued to struggle for a short time but ultimately lost the battle. The Meredith Village Players faced the same challenge; nevertheless, the true legacy of the organization is that it sparked a golden age of entertainment in Meredith that remains unmatched even today.

Chapter 9

Boy, Girl...Girl, Boy??

Then, when all in good time, Mrs. Montana presented him with his first son, Mr. Montana just clipped off the ever-pessimistic Jughead on the bottom half of the card, and mailed out the top half, with Archie's exuberant proclamation that Paige and Lynn Montana now have a little brother.
—Meredith News, *1955*

During the 1950s, Bob's life was chock-full with activities, and his schedule went far beyond demanding. The Meredith Village Players offered nonstop projects, he and Peg were busy with their girls and the popularity of *Archie* continued its rapid growth. Complex were the Montanas' days, yet the family was about to grow by one. Peg was pregnant with their third child.

It can be said that the couple was well prepared for the birth of the next little Montana. Bob was so prepared that he had created a birth announcement months in advance. Included in the announcement was both a boy's and a girl's name. Appearing on the top of the card was the name Raymond Douglas Montana, along with a drawing of Archie jumping for joy over the birth of a boy. Below was a girl's name, Therese Roberta Montana, accompanied by a drawing of a distressed Jughead, known for his strong dislike of girls.

The *Meredith News* published the birth announcement with a caption that read, "Most parents hope, but few dare say before a child is born whether it will be a boy or girl; practically no parent would go out and order birth announcements for the baby before the doctor told him what kind of

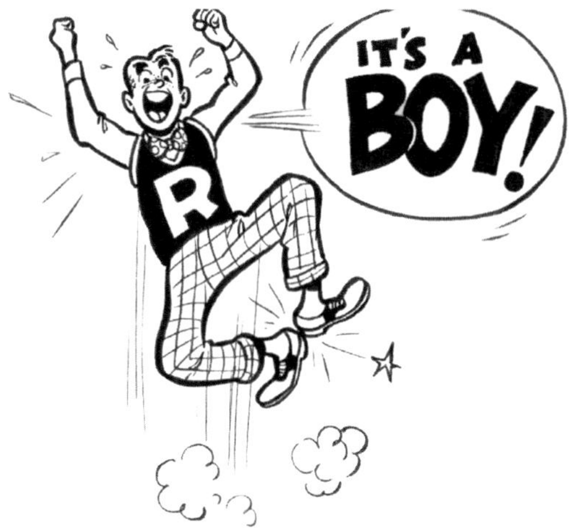

An exuberant Archie announces the birth of Bob and Peg's first-born son, Raymond. © *Montana family*.

baby it was."[28] However, Bob never failed to do things his own way. With the birth of Raymond Douglas Montana during the summer of 1955, Jughead was relieved, and the announcement with Archie enthusiastically jumping for joy went into the mail.

Archie may have proclaimed his exuberance over Raymond's arrival, but he was also occupied with spreading the news that the comic strip had moved from the McClure Syndicate to the King Features Syndicate. In January 1956, America's best-loved teenager and his creator became the subject of a full-page advertisement in *Editor and Publisher*. In the accompanying article, the cartoonist's life was put in a nutshell: "Bob's home is in Meredith, where he supports his wife, three children and a Model T Ford."[29]

Despite all the fanfare, Bob happily continued to work at home, and the smaller, more meaningful events that happened locally remained the focus of his attention. Early in 1956, the Laconia Key Club honored both Bob and Archie, making the dynamic duo honorary members. He attended their annual alumni banquet and sketched a beaming Archie for the spellbound members. The following month, the *Meredith News* reported that the Montanas hosted a birthday party for a local friend, which included skating on the Montana pond. A few weeks before that, Paige celebrated her seventh birthday with guests invited to a party at the Montanas'. These were the things that mattered, and they gave his life substance.

Bob never wished to become stagnant, and he possessed a constant desire to reach beyond his boundaries. His next goal was to try his hand at writing. In an instant, he became a published writer, as an article he penned appeared in *Archery* magazine. His witty writing style mirrored that of his cartooning style: exceedingly comical and always an exaggeration of reality. He chose to write about his introduction to the sport of archery in a 1956 article entitled "From Archie to Archery": "Working over a hot drawing board all day, grinding out my syndicated comic strip, *Archie*, is not always the healthy

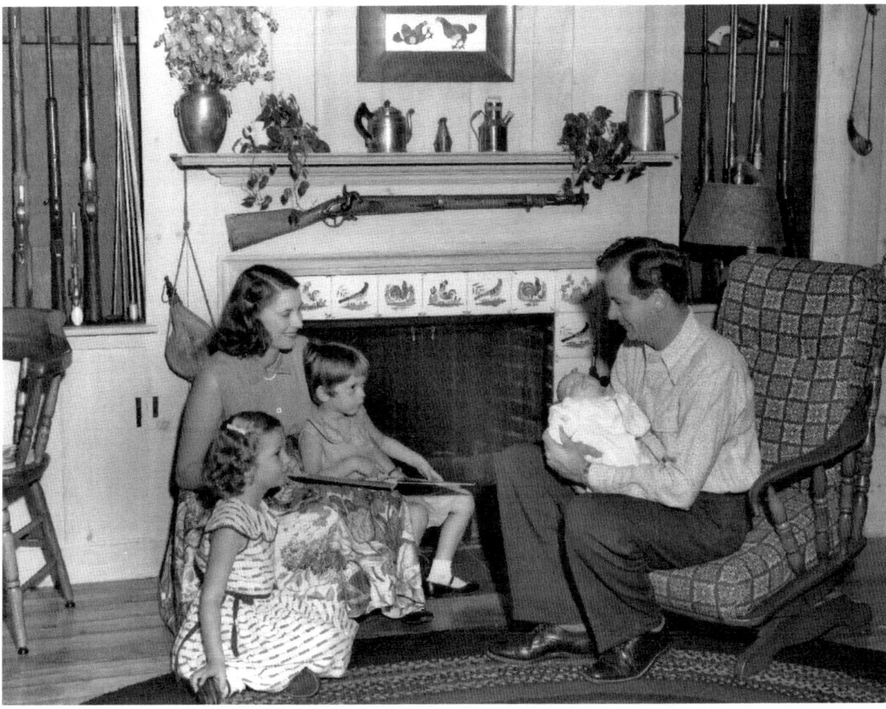

Peg with daughters Paige (left) and Lynn (right) look on as Bob holds Raymond. © *Montana family*.

racket most people think it is. About the only part of the body developed are the tricycle tires around one's middle."

He further tells the story of visiting the local sporting goods store, which in the article is run by Mr. Valliere. The Mr. Valliere he refers to is friend Bob Valliere, who was the owner of Bob's Texaco on Main Street in Meredith. Local entrepreneur Leander Pynn owned a sporting goods store in town at the time the article was written:

> *I followed his instructions like a good student, as he coached from a safe distance behind the counter. By the time I got the arrow drawn back to where the feathers tickled my nose, I was shaking like a belly dancer at the Folies Bergere.*
>
> *Suddenly, with a WHANG, BANG, CRASH, everything went black. It was some time before I could see well enough to find that the string had slipped off my artistic fingers, nearly taking the end of my nose with it. Mr. Valliere was on his hands and knees sweeping up the glass from his front door.*

> *In one sweeping wave of emotion, I was smitten with the archery bug. Here was a formidable weapon. A missile not to be sneezed at (even though my nose still stung). It gave a man a feeling of pioneer strength to send a shaft crashing through a glass door (removing all but the words "Sporting Goo") and plop up against the liquor store across the street. This was for me….*
>
> *My first night at the weekly indoor shoot was like walking into the Brooklyn Dodgers' Clubhouse straight from the rotary soft-ball team. It looked like everyone had been practicing for about forty years longer than I. The range was really a dance hall with a huge American flag at the end. The club had hung sheets of plywood in front of it, then an old 10 x 20 rug and straw bales in front of that with targets on them. My first arrow cleared the rug and stuck into a star in the top row of the flag. I felt like Benedict Arnold. The second shot hit low on the dance floor and skidded under the bales. This, I found later, was a cardinal sin equal to shooting the scorekeeper in the pants, because the club was allowed to use the hall only on their promise not to mar the dance floor. My most famous shot found a home in the upright piano.*
>
> *I bought two bales of straw to set up a butt next to my house and found that I can even lose arrows in an open field. I sent for catalogues, manuals, subscribed to* Archery *and read everything. We talked, ate and slept archery. I even wrote gags for my comic strip about archery, and my wife accused me of snapping the string on her pajamas in my sleep.*[30]

Bob had discovered both archery and writing, but the entire family was finding new hobbies at an alarming rate. During the 1950s, the Lakes Region was growing in leaps and bounds, and new activities were abundant. The *Archie* strip reflected this growth with a record number of local residents, places and events appearing during 1957. The same year, Bob drew the cover of the Meredith Firemen's Ball program, and shortly afterward, Betty and Archie showed up in the strip waltzing their way to a firemen's ball.

The cartoonist became a dedicated fan of water skiing as its growth soared. The sport found its way into the lives of many Lakes Region residents, and with the large amount of local support it received, the 1954 and 1959 National Championships were held on Lake Opechee in Laconia. As Bob's fascination with the water sport intensified, it made more splashes into the strip, as Archie and Jughead enjoyed their own water-skiing adventures. Strips featuring the art of skiing across water were guaranteed to show up each summer as Bob dusted off his water skis, tucked them under his arm and headed down to the lake.

In the winter, water skis were tucked away, and snow skis were pulled out and waxed. The Montana family was often seen at the Belknap Mountains Recreation Area in Gilford, one of the busiest ski areas in the state. During the winter seasons, *Archie* was filled with references to skiing and, more specifically, skiing at Belknap, which today is known as Gunstock.

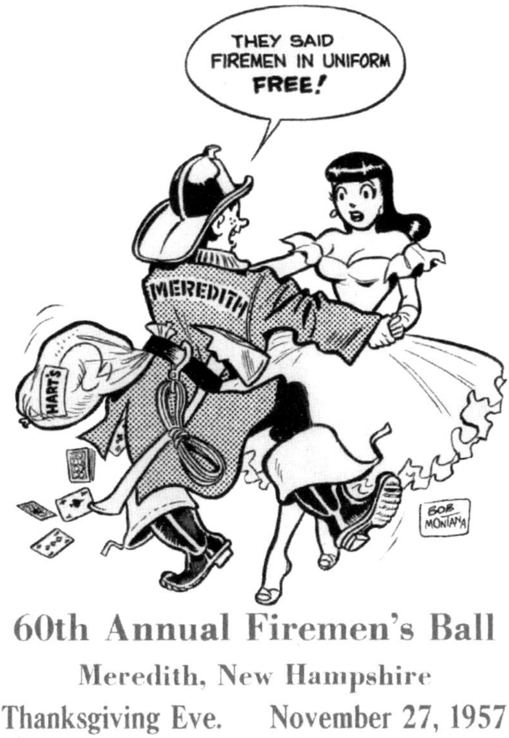

Archie and Veronica graced the cover of the Firemen's Ball program in 1957. © *Montana family*.

During the 1957–58 ski season, Jughead climbed up the Try-Me trail at the ski area and zipped down one of its four ski jumps on his ski bike. Archie and Veronica were seen going to a ski ball, an annual event held at the ski area's main lodge. Veronica and the gang enjoyed a little power shopping at the Arlberg Inn, snapping up the latest ski togs. The Montanas passed by the Arlberg each time they went skiing at Belknap, as it was conveniently located across from the main entrance.

Events and sports aside, Bob considered local businessmen a wonderful source for new characters. Big Buck Bucklin jumped wholeheartedly into the strip during the 1950s. Big Buck was a caricature of Vernal C. Bucklin, owner of Bucklin Tractor Company in Meredith. Once the large, muscular athlete appeared on the scene, Archie's life was never quite the same. Forever intent on beaning Archie, Big Buck chased the redheaded teenager through many of the strips, and each time, Archie had never failed to give him a good reason to be upset.

In the spring of 1958, Bob cut the ribbon and officially opened the new First National Supermarket on Route 3 in Meredith. Taking part in the ceremonies was storeowner, entrepreneur and civic leader Leander Pynn.

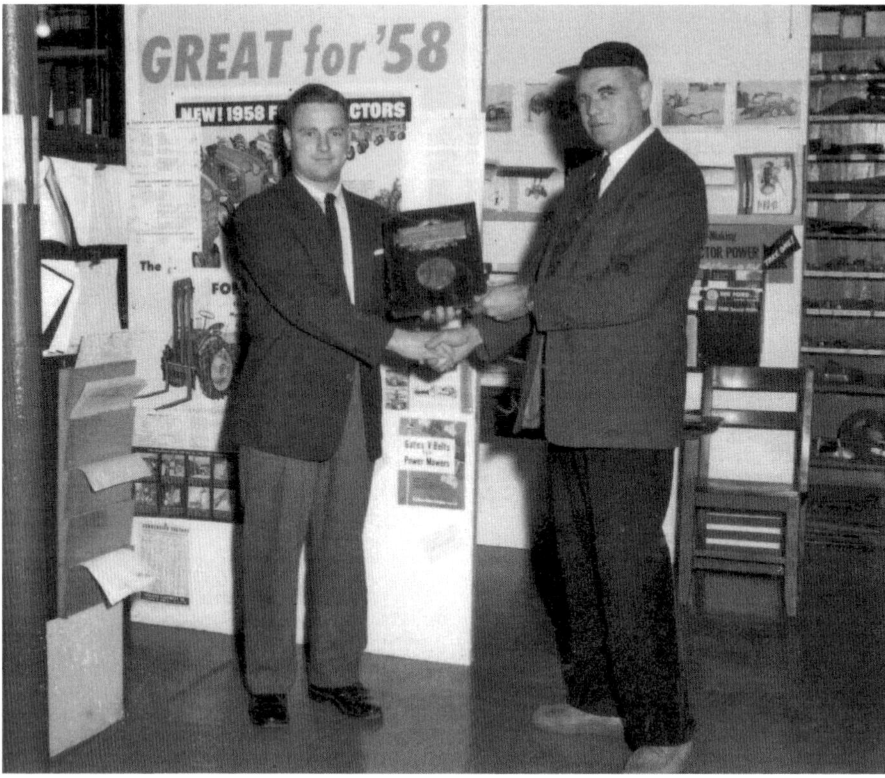

Vernal Bucklin (right), shown here in his store, appeared numerous times in *Archie* as Big Buck Bucklin. *Courtesy of Meredith Historical Society.*

The businessman had served as town selectman and moderator, but he was best known as the owner of Pynn's Garage. Leander opened the small business in 1920 and gave Bucklin Tractor Company its start by housing the fledgling business in his basement.

During the Depression, Pynn's employed twenty-five men and kept them busy with anything but car repairs and still managed to become the largest Ford agency north of Concord, New Hampshire. He sold the successful enterprise in 1951, only to start one business after another. Like Bucklin Tractor Company, Pynn's Garage caught the watchful eyes of Bob Montana. The garage was featured several times in *Archie*, but Bob cleverly renamed it Pins Garage.

As much as Bob loved the people and places in Meredith, his unique upbringing often made him long for the traveling days of his childhood. Fortunately, *Archie* could be drawn anywhere in the world as long as there

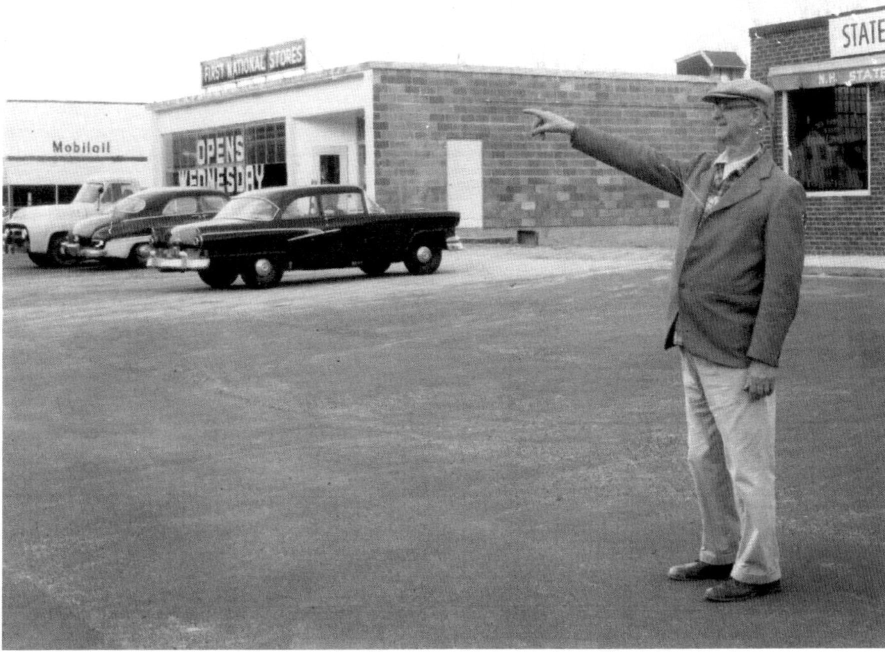

Leander Pynn stands in front of his First National store. Bob cut the ribbon at the store's grand opening. *Courtesy of Meredith Historical Society.*

was a mailbox nearby. Bob and his family took advantage of this benefit and embarked on several long-term stays in several countries. He wanted his children to learn about life in foreign lands by living a while in each, learning the language, tasting the food and, in general, soaking up the culture.

Chapter 10

A' Traveling We Will Go

When Bob decides it's time for a change of scene, we just pack up and go...it's no trouble really. We rented a house in Sussex and loved it. We have also lived in Mexico and in Rome, but we always come back to our house in Meredith.
—Peg Montana, September 1966

In September 1958, Meredith resident Robert Bacon and his family hosted a farewell luncheon for Bob, Peg, the kids and Roberta prior to their departure for an extended stay in Italy. After the party, the Montanas spent a night in New York City and then boarded the Italian liner *Gulio Casare*. It had always been Roberta's dream to visit Rome, the place of her birth. She was baptized in St. Peter's Cathedral and later crossed the Atlantic with her parents while still an infant. Fluent in Italian, she was the family's interpreter during their stay.

While the leaves in New England turned color, the Montanas happily set sail to the land of their ancestors. After acclimating to life in Italy, Roberta wrote a letter to the *Meredith News* in which she gave an update on the family's activities:

> *We are still enjoying Rome. I am learning to cook some real Italian dishes, which I hope to try out on my friends when I return. The open markets are full of oranges and tangerines and such things as artichokes and may greens, all coming from Naples and Sicily.*
>
> *I like Rome—I like all of Italy, and being able to speak Italian feels very much at home. I never miss a chance to visit in Italian with everyone I*

> *encounter, be it on the bus, with the portiere (door tender of our apartment) or the guards at museums and monuments. And they in turn are intrigued with an American who can speak Italian fluently. It all ends up generally by my having to explain that although I am an American, I was born in Rome and baptized in St. Peter. They then invariably say, "Ah! But you are a Roman." And I reply truthfully, "Yes, I am at heart." For even though I had not seen this native land of mine since I was nine months old, I find I have always had a dear spot in my heart for it. Therefore I think I am very lucky to be able to see it in my lifetime, thanks to my son.*[31]

Although their stay in Italy had a special purpose, the Montanas were excited to get back to Meredith during the summer of 1959. They returned home with a plethora of memories, and Bob returned sporting a beard. While away, he experimented with different styles of beards and moustaches, settling on the type everyone liked the most and then kept it for the rest of his life.

The Montanas' normal summer activities were enhanced by Bob agreeing to be a judge at the 1959 Miss Winnipesaukee Contest in the Weirs. In August, some of the largest crowds ever seen in Meredith jammed the streets and waterfront of the small community for the celebration of the 100th anniversary of the Meredith Village Fire District. Part of the celebration included the dedication of the new town docks in Meredith Bay. A large throng of onlookers stood along the bay awaiting the official dedication by Governor Wesley Powell. What the crowd did not know was that Bob had been planning and scheming, although those who knew him might have suspected he would find something comical in an otherwise serious situation. He and the crew of the *White Eagle* had already set sail straight toward the new docks by the time the crowd lined up on the shore. Bob and his fellow sailors were not there to be spectators but instead actors—actors that had a very large audience.

In a planned pre–ribbon-cutting skit, it was Peg Montana who stole the show as she made several frantic and humorous attempts to cut the ribbon prior to the actual ceremony. In doing so, she lost her balance, fell out of the boat in which she had been standing and plunged with a large splash into the waters of Meredith Bay. The crowd cheered as they showed their appreciation for the showmanship, and the *Meredith News* reported it as a "hilarious stunt" that got the formal festivities underway.[32]

One week prior to the celebration at the docks, Roberta's sister, Olga, and a friend visited from New York City. It was their first stay in New Hampshire,

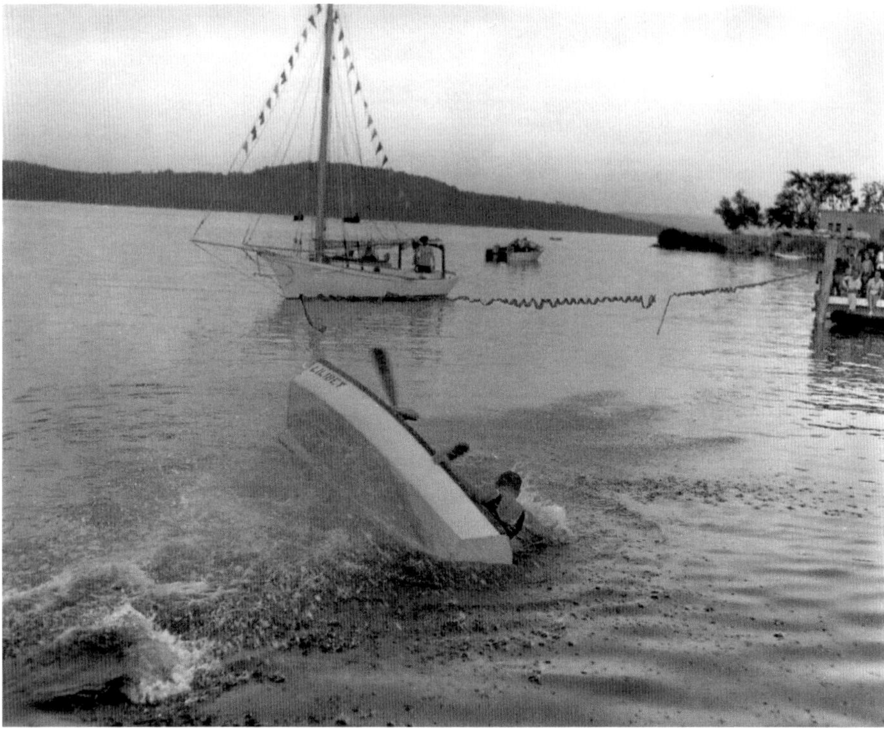

Peg Montana splashes into Meredith Bay as a fellow passenger holds on during a skit prior to the dock dedication. *Courtesy of Meredith Historical Society.*

and upon looking around at the open pastures, wooded hillsides and numerous lakes, they asked, "What do you find to do here?" Roberta decided that she would show them, taking the duo through the White Mountains up north, sailing around Lake Winnipesaukee on the motor ship *Mt. Washington* and visiting friends in town. At the end of the week, they attended the dock dedication. They left early on Monday morning, happy to be heading back to the city, this time saying that New Hampshire was no place for a peaceful vacation. Roberta simply replied, "They asked for it."[33]

By 1961, the Montana family was on the road again. Peg was expecting their fourth child when they arrived in Cuernavaca, Mexico. The trip coincided with Roberta making a permanent move to St. Petersburg, Florida, where Ruth was living. Despite the move, she forever thought of Meredith as her home, and there was no question she left a lasting impression on the town. She would, from time to time, visit New Hampshire and continued to write letters to the *Meredith News*.

By the time Roberta had settled into her new home and the Montanas were living in Mexico, the *Archie* comic strip appeared in over 430 newspapers throughout the world, including the *Mexican City Excelsior*. Bob was taken by the country and its people, and wanting to keep his writing skills sharp, he wrote a short article about the birth of his second son and his experiences in Mexico:

> *The Stork couldn't get our baby into that Mexican chimney! So Ray (6) stood by to catch his little brother in a "canasta."*
>
> *The baby came to our hacienda (where I work on* Archie*) shortly after we moved to Mexico from Meredith, New Hampshire. We named him (the baby, not the stork) Don Wherett Montana—the Wherett being my wife's maiden name. Then we discovered that here in Mexico, they add the wife's name to the end—so his birth certificate reads: Don Wherett Montana De Wherett!*
>
> *Our home is in Cuernavaca. It was an old pensone—done over by an architect with an artistic eye. There are seven bathrooms, a swimming pool with a fountain, a hammock and hot and cold running beetles....*
>
> *The studio is what sold us on the house. It has open-out windows on four sides. High above the surrounding trees and bougainvillea, it has a view of the two great snow-capped mountains: Popo and The Sleeping Lady. Here I work on* Archie *until noon. Then a plunge into the pool and lunch of tacos, cassadias and a good cervesa corona by the pool. Then back to work or a ride—often going back to work in the cool of the evening.*
>
> *The Mexican people have a quick wit and like to laugh. We've made lots of good friends below the border.*[34]

By June 1961, Bob, Peg and their children—now numbering four—had arrived home in Meredith. It was almost as if fate had planned for the Montana family to imitate *Archie* so closely. After the birth of Donald, the young main characters in both the family and the strip were two girls and two boys. Archie's influence was everywhere.

The Montanas utilized the summer to unwind, enjoy life on the farm and make the adjustment to the family being larger by one. Bob's assistant, Ruth Harding, became an adored friend to all four of the Montana children in addition to helping their father with *Archie*. She was affectionately known as "Foofie" to them, appearing in the strip bearing that name, and on one occasion, she stepped in as a date for Jughead.

While Paige and Lynn went back to school in the fall, Raymond was busy with his own project. He entered his poultry in the Sandwich Fair. The

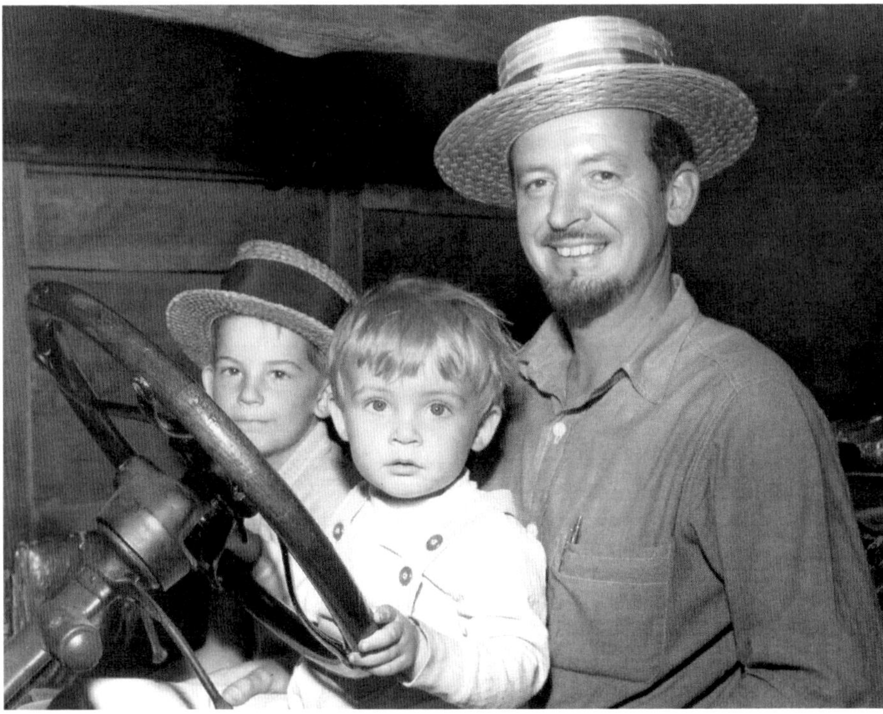

Bob in 1962 with sons Ray (left) and Don. © *Montana family*.

fair is held each October in the nearby town of Sandwich and is enjoyed by thousands. Started in 1886, it stands strong as a symbol of a typical New England agricultural fair.[35] The fair was one of Bob's favorites, and when Raymond placed his poultry and pigeons into the fair, he won big, as reported in the *Meredith News*:

> *The Sandwich Fair was a thrilling occasion for six-year-old Raymond Montana, whose poultry and pigeons reaped a harvest of awards. He brought home three blue ribbons; his black sex-link pullet winning 1st prize and champion, his golden pullet winning 1st prize, and his pair of White King homing pigeons, 1st prize. Raymond, son of Mr. and Mrs. Bob Montana, arises early each morning to care for his pets before he leaves to attend first grade at Lang Street School.*[36]

Fall fairs and frosts gave way to winter snow, which in turn brought spring to the Lakes Region. Bob had been invited to New York City to attend

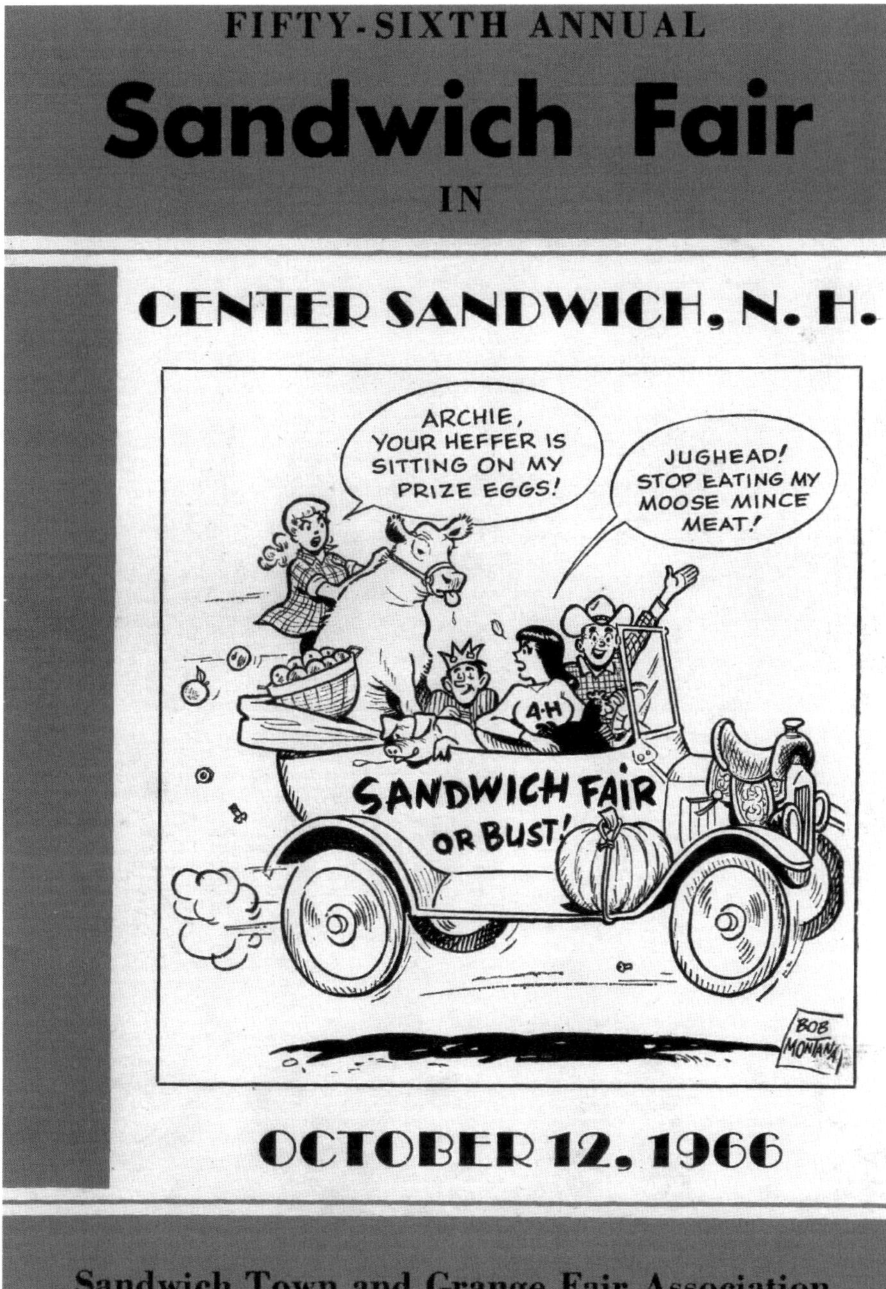

The 1966 Sandwich Fair program cover was designed by Bob Montana, one of the fair's biggest fans. © *Montana family*.

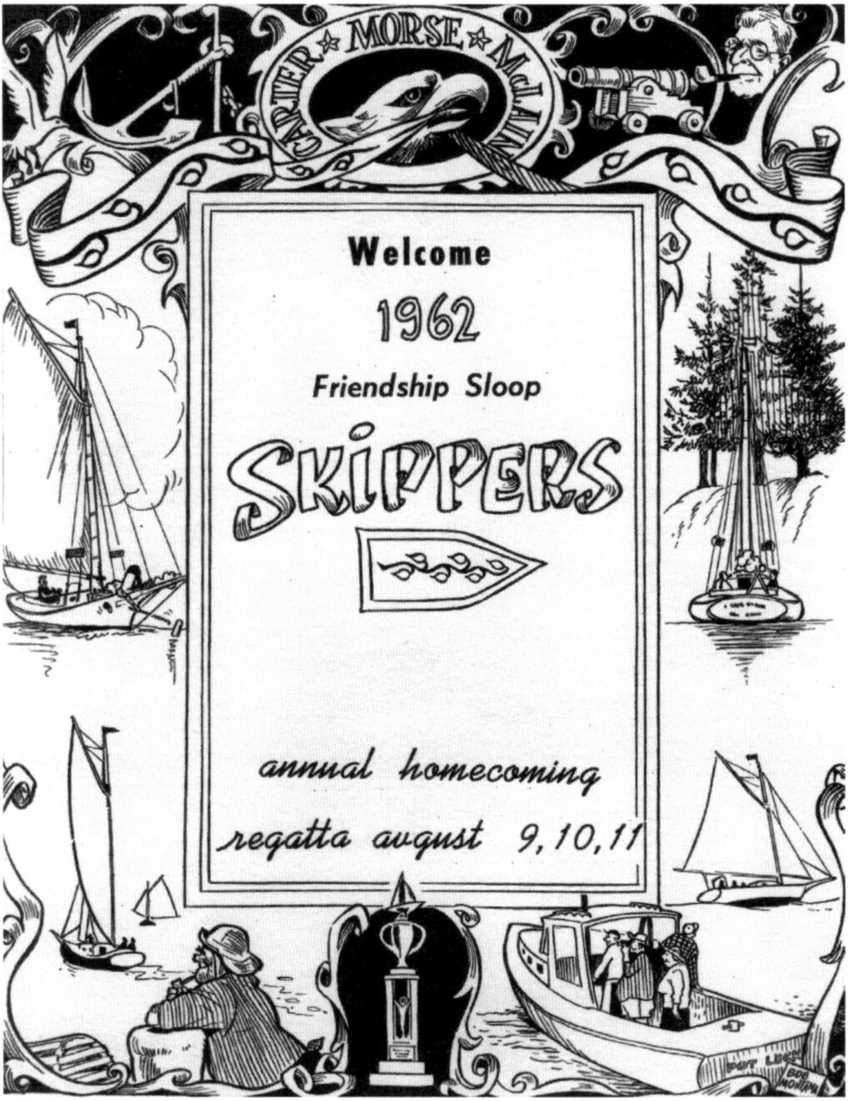

As a member of the Winnipesaukee Yacht Club, Bob designed the 1962 Annual Homecoming Regatta cover. © *Montana family*.

the first International Cartoonists Convention sponsored by the National Cartoonists Society. The entire family traveled to the Big Apple to attend the event and experience one of the highlights of the convention: Times Square being renamed Cartoonist's Square for one day. The climax of the convention was the awards dinner at the Astor Ballroom.

In August, they attended the 1962 Annual Regatta in Friendship, Maine, which Bob and twenty-one other skippers had planned the previous fall while in Marblehead, Massachusetts. A group representing the Winnipesaukee Yacht Club participated; Bob was a competitor and missed winning the cup by a small margin. Back home on Lake Winnipesaukee, the Montanas' *White Eagle* had become so well known that it had turned into the most photographed boat on the lake.

The following spring, in 1963, the Meredith Village Players reappeared on the scene. An announcement came that the group planned to present a new production, the *20th Century Review*. This production was different than their previous plays of the 1950s; it would be a joint effort between the Players and the music department at Inter-Lakes High School. The school's music supervisor, Bruce Heald, had moved to Meredith several years prior and was working to create a bigger and better music department.

The two groups met at the Montana home to select the musical numbers and skits to be used in the production. Tom Kemp and Bruce Heald were chosen as directors. The production came together quickly, and the *Meredith News* was proud to run the announcement:

> *A program of gaiety, laughs and fun is assured Saturday evening at the Robert Pottle Memorial Auditorium, where the Meredith Village Players will present "20th Century Review," a vaudeville show featuring songs, dances and customs through the 1900s to the present day.*
>
> *Skits and songs will be presented by many of the famous stars of the Players. George and Isabelle Russell will present a hilarious skit depicting life in a New York apartment in 1905. "The Way You Look Tonight," starring Janet Grad, Peg Montana and Beverly Bacon, will keep the audience howling with laughter...that talented and versatile pair "Hank" and "Hobie" Stark will be seen in "The Park," a feature sure to bring down the house. "End of the Beginning," starring Raymond Roux, Herman and Greg Olsen and Pierce and Dot Edmonds, is another skit that is one of the funniest ever dreamed up by the versatile Players.*
>
> *The scintillating "Montana Dance Combo" will render novelty selections that will be a topic of conversations for months to come. Members of the combo are Bob Montana, Alan Israel, Will and Linden Grad and Rene DeLathauwer, with George Russell doing the dancing bit.*[37]

The combination production ranked among one of the best the town had witnessed, and as an added bonus, it gave Bob fodder for his comic strip.

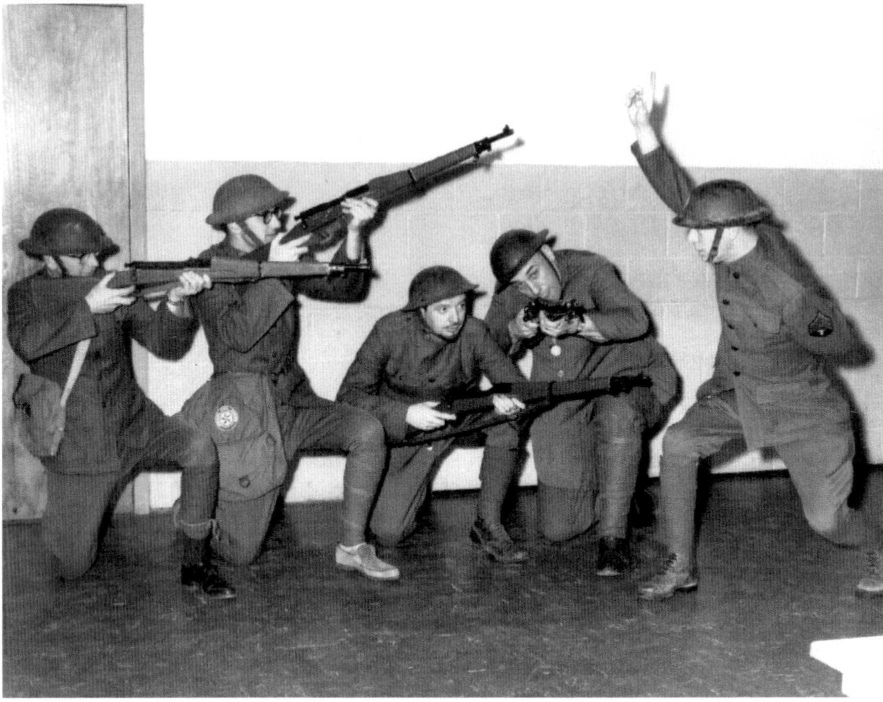

Linden Grad, Alan Israel, Bob Montana, Philip Swett and Will Grad as Doughboys in the *20th Century Review*. © *Montana family*.

Two of the men involved in the production just so happened to land up in *Archie*. Alan Israel, a pharmacist in town, appeared as himself in the strip, while Bruce Heald appeared as a music conductor. In one strip, Archie and the gang were happily involved in a band boosters fundraising event.

Seeing the potential for raising funds for worthy organizations, the Players and Inter-Lakes met again at Bob's home, and another production was planned for the following February. The proceeds from the show were to be split equally between the Inter-Lakes High School band and the Meredith Library Association. Not unlike the *20th Century Review* of the previous spring, the two-night show they planned would be a slapstick comedy. Tom Kemp and Bruce Heald returned as directors.

A month before the show, members of the Village Players and Inter-Lakes High School were rehearsing together, and the *Meredith News* reported that confusion seemed to reign. Numbers were being written and rewritten. Dancers were practicing daily. Director Tom Kemp assured the reporters that all was coming along as planned. He added that he and his crew were working on special lighting for this year's production, a change from the previous year.

During the two-night run, all attendance records were broken. Well over four hundred people attended the first night's show, and nearly five hundred attended the second. Bob Bennett, a columnist for the *Meredith News*, popular square-dance caller and a close friend to Bob Montana, recalled that wild production in his column, "I Remember When":

> *On another occasion, Bob teamed up with Bruce Heald, the high school band director, in putting on a two-night gala…that was a weekend to remember. I still laugh about some of the things that went on.*
>
> *One segment was a skit by Bob, Will Grad, Linden Grad, Phil Swett and Alan Israel. They played instruments for a couple of numbers, Bob with his homemade "jazz stick," a trumpet, a saxophone, a clarinet and a string bass. They really put out beautiful music in that skit. I had a small part in this feature; one of the skits they pulled was with a group dressed as WWI Doughboys. They horsed around, and Bob pulled out what looked like a hand grenade. He acted like he pulled the pin and tossed it to Will Grad, Will tossed it to Linden like it was a hot potato, Lin chucked it to Phil Swett, and Phil threw it back to Bob, who acted like he threw it out over the audience. That was my cue. I was in the entrance foyer with a small cannon charged with black powder. When Bob reared back to simulate his throw, I lit the wick on the cannon, and seconds later, the cannon went off with a resounding "Bang!" The whole audience must have jumped a foot off their chairs, it startled them so. When the realization set in, it brought the house down. He always found humor in things that he did.*[38]

Bob Bennett was correct. No matter where Bob was or what he was doing, he could find the humor in it; he would always choose to look toward the positive side of any situation. His endless optimism saw him through many tough times in life. It also guided him through nerve-racking situations, especially one that occurred during the next trip the Montana family took abroad.

Chapter 11

To England...and Back

It's been a mild winter here in Southern England. I have a nice studio on the third floor with a view of the River Ouse, with its swans gliding by, and where I turn out Archie *every week...life is very easy and peaceful here. Nevertheless, we miss the farm and our friends in New Hampshire.*

—Bob Montana, 1965

In the fall of 1964, the Montana family prepared for their next adventure abroad. Bob first made a quick trip to the 1964 World's Fair before they all embarked on a lengthy stay in England. The *Meredith News* shared the information with its readers:

> *Bob Montana is accompanying "Archie" and friends on a flying trip to the World's Fair in New York on Friday, down and back the same day. This is sort of a command performance, with Bob commissioned to make a tape which will be shown on color TV in the Cavalcade of Comics at the RCA pavilion at the Fair. With Bob, besides "Archie" and gang, will be his famous jazz stick. After the Fair closes, RCA plans to put the taped show out over the networks, and it may also be made into a short color movie. Bob's wife, Peggy, and four children—Paige, Lynn, Raymond and Donald—will remain home this time, as they are busy packing for their forthcoming trip to England. They leave Meredith on Aug. 31 and sail Sept. 2 on the* Queen Mary. *For the next year, they will live in South Hampton in Sussex. The children are already enrolled in school over there.*[39]

Before the Montanas left, the C. Paul Reeds of Meredith threw a farewell party with thirty-five guests. The Reeds then accompanied the family to New York, where they all spent two days together before boarding the *Queen Mary*. Prior to the Reeds returning home to Meredith, they stayed for a small and intimate on-board party. As for *Archie*, which was published in over 550 newspapers, Bob said, "We might even let him take a trip in the strip showing up in England and also on the Continent."[40]

By October, they were settled into a comfortable, four-hundred-year-old house in the middle of Sussex, and their picturesque neighborhood included two windmills named Jack and Jill. As much as Bob enjoyed life in England, he missed his home in Meredith and sent a letter to the *Meredith News*:

> *We certainly enjoy getting the "News" over here—and when the Royal Mail pops it under our door, tea is spilled, crumpets are trampled and the coal scuttle overturned in the mad rush to lay hands on it first! We are very happy with this house; very comfortable with complete central heat from automatic oil (just like home), a coal range in the kitchen and four fireplaces. Today (Jan. 15) was bright and sunny, in the 40s. The forsythia is in blossom, and the trees are beginning to bud—so winter is nearly over. (However, it is raining tonight as I sit and write this and watch the BBC News.)*[41]

Life in England may have been easy and peaceful, but those words can hardly be used to describe the return trip home. In April 1966, the family began their journey back home via Rome, where they had arrived by train. Their frightful crossing of the Atlantic Ocean was one that would make national headlines.

On April 12, the *Michelangelo* and its passengers became battered after getting caught in a storm nearly 1,500 miles from New York. Enormous waves caused heavy damage to the nearly fifty-thousand-ton vessel, breaking windows, twisting heavy steel and damaging the ship's superstructure. Three passengers were killed. One crew member later died in a hospital from his injuries. Another crew member was severely injured and had to be airlifted; seven crew members and five passengers were also injured.

During the storm, the ship's executive officer, Captain Claudio Cosulich, was high in the bridge of the almost nine-hundred-foot ship, over eighty feet above the water line. Rogue waves sent tons of water crashing into the heavy protective glass windows, causing the captain and his crew to be hit with flying pieces of shattered glass. Captain Cosulich recounted the storm when he talked with reporters after his ship, flags flying at half-staff, docked in New York:

> *I have been 41 years at sea, and it was the most severe I have experienced. Full preparations for a storm had been made. Lifelines were extended, portholes were battened tight, speed was reduced to 16 knots, and the crew began securing everything they could. I cannot close now without a word of praise for my officers and crew. They performed their duties well. These are not mere words. They acted in the best tradition of the men who go to sea.*
>
> *And I must mention the bravery of my passengers. They followed orders. There was no panic. They have made me proud in a situation over which neither we nor they had any control.*[42]

Reporters were eager to interview Bob Montana as well. He gave them a brief description of what had happened, as he explained, "The waves looked like apartment buildings. I was worried about how much the ship could take. The ship was not just rolling and pitching; it shuddered. Things jumped. Everything fell onto the floor, even the telephones." He finished the interview by firmly stating, "The next cabin I reserve will be a log cabin in New Hampshire."[43]

Bob's daughter, Lynn, was fourteen at the time and still has vivid memories of the ill-fated crossing. She recalled the details of the voyage:

> *We went through a storm—about 24 hours or so—and it was very windy. Our ship received a mayday call from another ship, and we had to head toward it, which caused us to go right back into the storm, and it had intensified. The ship shuddered because it would rise to the top of a high wave, and the propellers would literally come out of the water.*
>
> *Most of the waves were estimated at approximately forty-five feet, but there was one wave that was over seventy-five feet, which hit the upper decks. The ship was taking on water but was able to continue to New York. One steward had both legs crushed and had to be airlifted when we finally docked.*
>
> *All the passengers were locked in certain sections of the ship so that it was easier for the crew to watch them. My sister, Paige, wasn't with us, as she had gone to see a movie in the ship's cinema. She was scared because she was separated from us, but the crew assured us that everyone in the cinema was fine.*

> *My father was such a great person to have around in a crisis. We were in a small section of the ship, and most were Americans. My father always carried a harmonica in his pocket, so he took it out, and while he played it, the rest of us sang.*
>
> *Once we docked in New York, the passengers were kept on board for a number of hours and then were allowed to walk around the deck to view the damage. I'll never forget that sight—the heavy pieces of metal shredded into small pieces.*[44]

In August 1966, Bob revisited memories of that trip when he drew Jughead and Archie experiencing a rough ride on a ship. Jughead, who is shown taking pictures, quickly changes the film to color so that he can capture Archie's green face. Bob had the amazing ability to find humor in all things—including his own harrowing journey on the high seas.

That trip would be the last the family took together before Paige and Lynn went off to different schools. Lynn enrolled as a student at Cushing Academy in Ashburnham, Massachusetts, and quickly made the honors list. In June 1967, Paige graduated from Inter-Lakes High School, but Bob continued to support the local band boosters and enjoyed creating caricatures of the president and vice-president of the Inter-Lakes High School Band.

In the fall, Paige enrolled as a freshman at Garland College in Boston, and soon afterward, she invited Bob to attend the school's annual Fathers' Weekend. During the week, he was in New York City to attend a cartoonists' sport night at the Hotel Commodore. By Saturday, he was with Paige and her classmates at a Harvard-Dartmouth football game celebrating Fathers' Weekend.

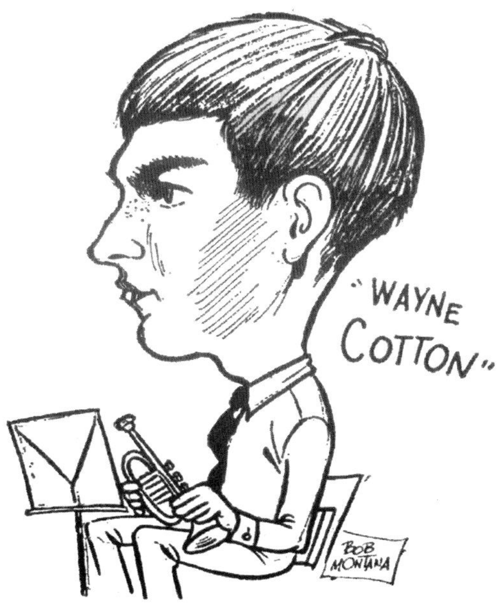

Every year, Bob drew caricatures of the president and vice-president of the Inter-Lakes High School band. © *Montana family*.

With both the girls off at school, Peg and Bob took in

a young French au pair named Marie. She assisted Peg with the care of the boys and in the process learned how to farm. Living with the Montana family was a life-changing experience for her, as she later explained:

> *Bob and Peggy invited me to stay with them after I left a family in Boston where I was an au pair girl. I was nineteen then. At that time, Lynn and Paige were going away to university, and Peggy needed to have company and someone to take care of Ray and Donald. Peggy was a good teacher to me. I had never lived on a farm before, so it was wonderful for me to discover and learn the basics of good living.*
>
> *After this first stay at the Montana's, I went back twice. Then, Lynn came to France to study art, and we shared an apartment. Bob was an exquisite person, as was his wife. They had the intelligence of mixing artwork and intellectual activities with friends and farm life. Everything I learned with them, I use in my life in France, where I've a country house and a big garden.*
>
> *Before I left them, though I had my plane ticket, they told me to give it to someone, and they offered me the ticket to go back on the* France, *because it was one of the last crossings of that wonderful ship. We drove to New York, and they accompanied me to my room, where a bottle of champagne (that they had ordered ahead) was waiting for us.*[45]

In April 1968, Bob was nominated by the National Cartoonists Society for the Outstanding Cartoonist of the Year Award, also known as the Reuben Award. Over six hundred members of the society voted to nominate him, along with Charles Schulz, creator of *Peanuts*, and Johnny Hart, co-creator of the *Wizard of Id*. The cartoonists went through two rounds of voting before the winner was chosen, and that year, the Reuben went to Johnny Hart for the *Wizard of Id*.

To Bob, that didn't matter—life continued on. In 1969, Paige graduated from college and Lynn graduated from Cushing Academy. In September, Archie had broken into the field of television with his own Saturday morning show on CBS, and a new song, "Sugar, Sugar," which was based on the comic, rocketed up the charts to number one. It seemed as if there wasn't anything else for Bob or Archie to achieve.

During the interview for his National Cartoonists Society profile, Bob was asked to describe his occupation. His reply was, "Wife and four children." Asked if he had a hobby, he replied, "*Archie*, since 1941." When quizzed about what awards he had received, his answer was brief and to the point: "My children."[46]

At first glance, one might think Bob was attempting to be humorous with his answers. In reality, he might have been plainly (and honestly) describing how he felt about his life. His family was his main occupation, and no matter what award he did or did not receive, his wife and his children remained the center of his life.

Chapter 12

In and About Meredith

Actually, Archie and Jughead and the rest of the crew are no longer youngsters in the matter of time; but they continue to hold their own against Batman and the Beatles, furnishing spontaneous and wholesome humor which brings a smile to readers everywhere. And, best of all, it starts right here in Meredith.
—Meredith News, *November 1966*

In and About Meredith," the popular section in the *Meredith News* that included the latest neighborhood gossip, offered the best glimpse into life in Meredith. Bob Montana enjoyed traveling with his family, but the world outside of New Hampshire was not the source of his inspiration. He thrived in Meredith, and it generated endless situations and notions for him to include in *Archie*. In an interview for *Cartoonist PROfiles*, he explained the source of his inspiration:

> *Well, I get lots of ideas from things I've done myself. I guess I was impressed with some advice given by Ernest Hemingway to the effect that you do your best writing about things you're familiar with. I take up every sport, even if only temporary—and I probably do more along this line than I should. Whether it happens to be water skiing, sailing or what have you, I get a lot of gags from these activities. I'm basically interested in people and everything around me.*[47]

Residents and friends in Meredith had their own somewhat crazy adventures, and all were carefully observed by Bob Montana. Dentist Dr.

Deneault proved to be a never-ending source of humor and inspiration, as reported in the paper:

> *Dr. Frederick J. Deneault has been quite busy during the past few weeks trying to discourage the pigeons that moved to the roof and eves of his home from similar quarters at the Dr. Herman Olsen home. Dr. Deneault has been annoying the pigeons with a slingshot, an art at which he has become quite proficient, at every opportunity. But the pigeons refused to become discouraged and even brought their friends to enjoy their luxurious new quarters. Sunday evening their constant coo-ing and messy habits got to be too much for Doc Deneault to take any longer, so with the aid of Dr. Olsen and under the supervision of Chief of Police Carroll Straw, the pigeon nuisance was done away with, forever Dr. Deneault hopes. However, the powerful flashlight that was used during "Operation Pigeon" and three men moving around in the darkness upset and frightened a lady neighbor so much that she put in a call for police assistance.*[48]

The simple, straightforward and mostly rural lifestyle in Meredith had its own unique style of humor, described in the following story that became front-page news:

> *A pig that a-wandering went upsetting residents of the Neal Shore section for several days has found a good home at the farm of Mr. and Mrs. Reuben Corliss in Meredith Center. No one knows where the 40-pound porker came from, but it is surmised that it fell off a passing truck. So far no one has claimed the adventuring pig.*
>
> *Chief Norman Martin was called by an irate lady Saturday to remove the invading porker from a shed near her home. Although an unusual request, Chief Martin was equal to the task, captured the squealing pig with dispatch and loaded it in the back seat of the police cruiser. The pig rode in style to the Martin home, where it spent the night in the cellar.*
>
> *Being host for one night to the squealing pig was more than enough for the Martin family, so suitable quarters were found early the next morning at the Corliss farm, where it is now enjoying the comfort of accustomed surroundings and the company of the other farm animals.*[49]

The *Archie* comic strip was filled with the Lakes Region. One day, Bob might add in Meredith's postmaster, Ray Huckins, and have Jughead work him over with a zip code that included a fraction. The next day, he would

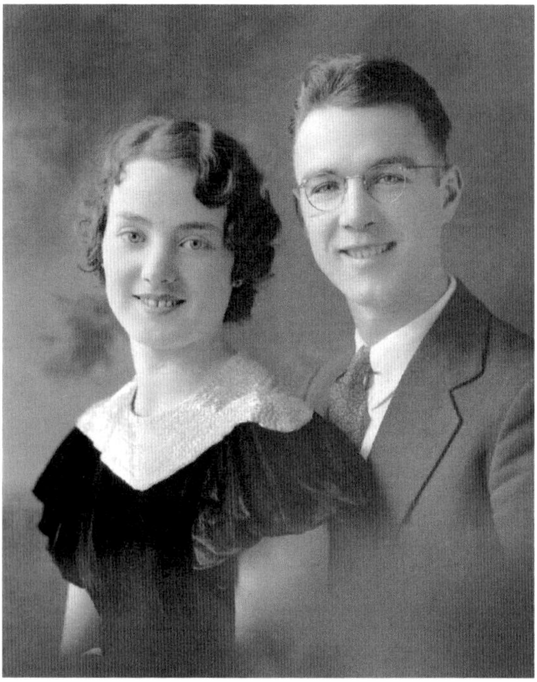

Owner of Allen Barber Shop, Jesse Allen, and his wife, Violet, circa 1935. *Courtesy of Meredith Historical Society.*

add in Mrs. Rouvali's famous macaroni salad (one of his personal favorites) by having it appear at a potluck supper at Riverdale High. Daughter Lynn was the star of a Sunday *Archie* after she broke her leg while skiing at Gunstock and was shown in the strip wearing a cast. Meredith businesses Harry's Oil, the Yarnery, Bacon's Self-Serve Laundry and Prescott Lumber all became part of *Archie* at one time or another.

Allen Barber Shop, owned and operated by Jesse Allen, was the most important gathering spot in Meredith and one that was carefully watched by Bob. It was a place for discussions and debates, with a haircut and shave often secondary. The shop was first opened in 1911 by Jesse's father, Chester, and after serving in World War II, Jesse took over the reins. He became the town historian and, over the years, amassed a large collection of historical items, which were proudly displayed in the shop. Jesse and his popular barbershop were drawn into *Archie* several times.

Life in this typical New England town may have appeared idyllic from the outside. Like other towns, Meredith struggled with its own problems. The more complex society became, the more complicated the issues. In 1955, the town's biggest concern was how to deal with the canal that ran through the center of town. As a mill town, it had relied on waterpower, and the canal was a critical part of its lifeline. By the 1950s, the need for waterpower was long gone, and the canal had developed into nothing more than a safety hazard. Beyond the worry of someone falling into it, the growing number of cars and downtown businesses caused a need for more parking.

Committee reports recommended covering parts of the canal in order to create those much-needed parking spaces and installing a safety fence. The

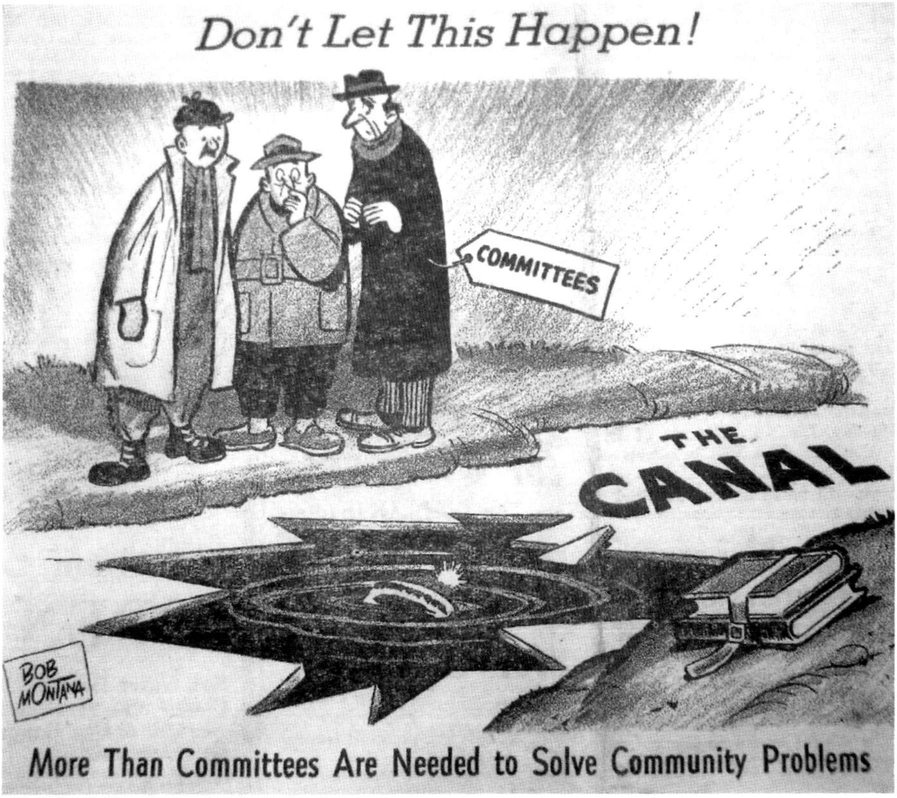

Meredith's canal dilemma is depicted by Bob in this editorial cartoon, which accompanied an article in the *Meredith News*. © *Montana family*.

committee did its part; it was up to the residents to resolve the issue at the next town meeting. Bob helped get the message out by doing what he did best; his cartoon appeared on the front page of the *Meredith News*, which illustrated the need for action from the residents.

Meredith and neighboring Center Harbor were two towns trying to adapt to the increasing population, the growing number of schoolchildren and overcrowding in the classrooms. Officials from both towns worked together, and after many meetings and discussions, they agreed to send their students to a central school. Bob breezed in with a front-page drawing that depicted the cooperation between the towns and the benefit to the children.

In the spring of 1960, Meredith continued to deal with rapid and extensive changes. The resurfacing of Main Street had begun, and prior to the start of the project, two large elms were removed. By the end of the year, the town found itself in the middle of a debate as it grappled with the rapidly

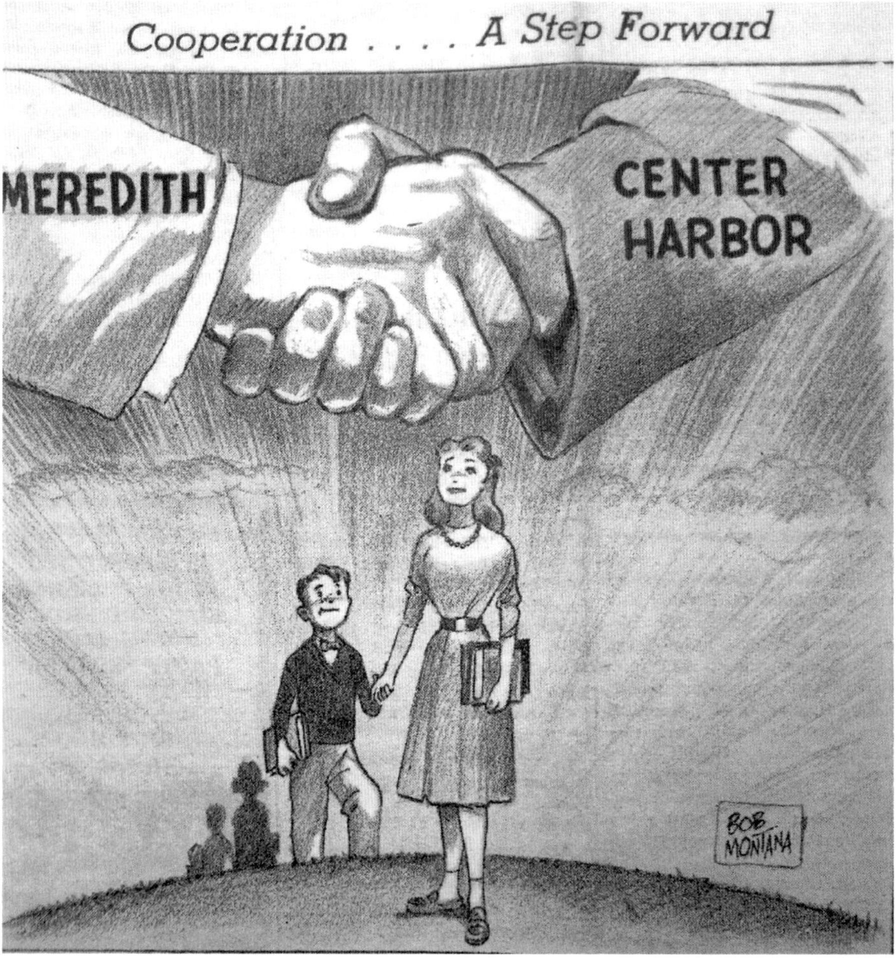

Bob's talent as an illustrator shines in this drawing depicting the cooperation of several towns regarding a school issue. © *Montana family*.

increasing volume of traffic on narrow Main Street. Two century-old elms near the library had begun to create a nagging problem for the board of selectmen. Residents were divided evenly on whether to remove the trees that had become a hazard to the ever-increasing amount of traffic or preserve their graceful beauty. A momentary solution was the installation of granite curbs that provided protection for the trees but reached far into the road. Residents then considered the curbs even more of a traffic problem, so the granite slabs were removed.

The following spring, the elms were cut down. The majority of residents admitted that the action upset them, especially since they knew the trees had watched over the activities of Main Street for nearly a century. Dutch elm disease was claiming other trees at an alarming rate, but these trees had been removed in the name of progress. The elimination of the large elms left a large, unsightly area, causing town officials to put out a call for an organization to replant trees in a more suitable location.

Bob was watching and pondering the tree dilemma carefully as he went about his usual business. He agreed with residents that felt the rapid loss of trees was causing Meredith to lose its quaint, small-town look. As always, Bob dealt with the changes in Meredith in his own way and in his own time.

However, his intense interest in his hometown was set aside when he ventured out into the Lakes Region, and it was guaranteed that some of what he saw and experienced outside of Meredith would be stitched into *Archie*. Laconia's classic old theater, the Colonial, the impressive O'Shea's department store and Mr. Veazey of the city's building supply store, Boulia-Gorrell, gained their own spotlight in the strip.

One of the stores Bob and his family frequented was Piche's, a sports shop in nearby Gilford. It was the place where they bought ski equipment, both Alpine and Nordic. Francis Piche established the business during the 1930s, worked

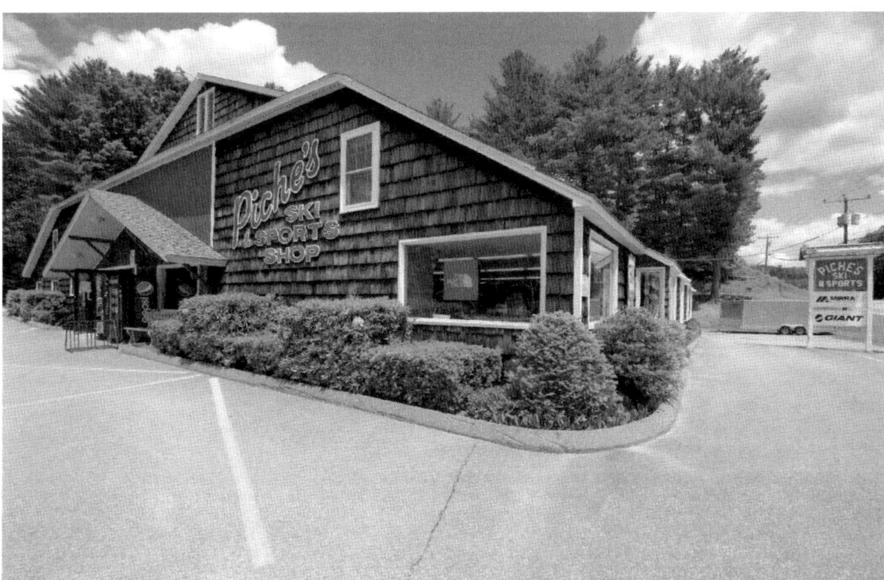

Piche's, a favorite Lakes Region sports shop, fitted the Montana family with skis. *Photo by Harrison Haas.*

out of his home and then expanded into a commercial property in Gilford. He eventually sold the establishment to his long-time assistant, Bob Bolduc.

When Bob stopped in, he looked for ski equipment—and ideas. In a 1963 strip, Archie and Jughead paid a visit to the store, complaining that both sets of their mismatched skis consisted of one ski being longer than the other. Bob Bolduc looked forward to the times when the great cartoonist came in to visit, as he explained during an interview:

> *Bob Montana would come into the store quite often, and over the years, we sold him plenty of skis, mostly cross-country. He was a great guy, extremely down-to-earth, and the latest trends in ski equipment didn't faze him; he liked the simpler designs.*
>
> *He'd come in and say to me, "Come on, Bob, give me some food!"—meaning he was looking for inspiration. So, I would tell him all sorts of stories, mostly from my childhood growing up on the Bolduc farm here in town.*
>
> *He did feature Piche's in the comic strip during the 60s, and he introduced me to Dick Brooks, who drew the* Jackson Twins *strip. Bob was a wonderful guy and one that was completely unaffected by being a celebrity. I always enjoyed talking with him.*[50]

In 1964, Bob Montana came together with local businessman Bob Lawton when the two men volunteered as trustees of the Meredith Public Library. Mr. Lawton was owner of the newly opened Funspot in the Weirs. The business had its roots in the popular Weirs Sports Center, which began as a small arcade and miniature golf course. Bob Lawton opened the business in 1952 at the age of twenty-one and later formed a partnership with his brother, John. Under the management of the talented brothers, the arcade grew to become the world's largest.[51]

In 1965, Bob Lawton wanted to have a new and unique logo created for Funspot, and he asked Bob Montana to design it. That year, the cartoonist's jester logo was introduced to the public as the new face of Funspot. As it might be expected, the jester had a connection to *Archie*: Bob modeled the image after Archie's best pal, Jughead. Fifteen years later, when Funspot's new game token was introduced, the jester appeared on the back, and it remains there today.

While Laconia's grand arcade enjoyed its new logo, as well as several appearances in Archie, Meredith residents were preoccupied with the elimination of more trees. Two diseased but stately elms were removed from in front of the Seneca Ladd house, which was more than a century old.

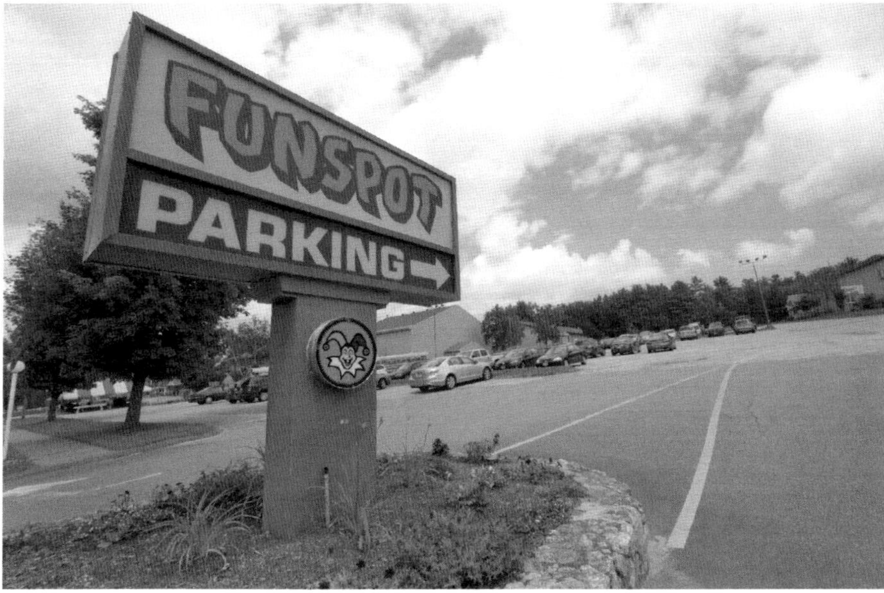

Above: Funspot, the world's largest arcade, was started by businessman Robert Lawton. *Photo by Harrison Haas.*

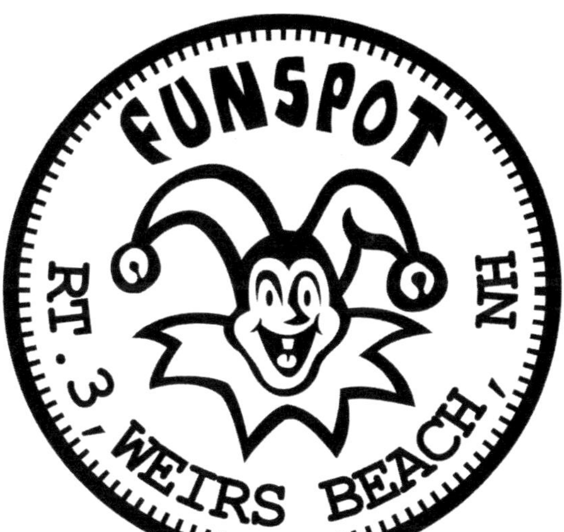

Right: The jester logo created by Bob for Funspot was modeled after the *Archie* character Jughead. *Courtesy of Robert Lawton.*

It was estimated that Mr. Ladd, first treasurer and one of the founders of the Meredith Village Savings Bank, had planted the trees during the 1850s. With the vast number of trees being removed from the village landscape, residents were worried that the beauty and charm of their community had been lost forever. Once again, residents agreed that what was needed was a person or group to organize an effort to replace the lost shade trees. But no one stepped forward to handle the task.

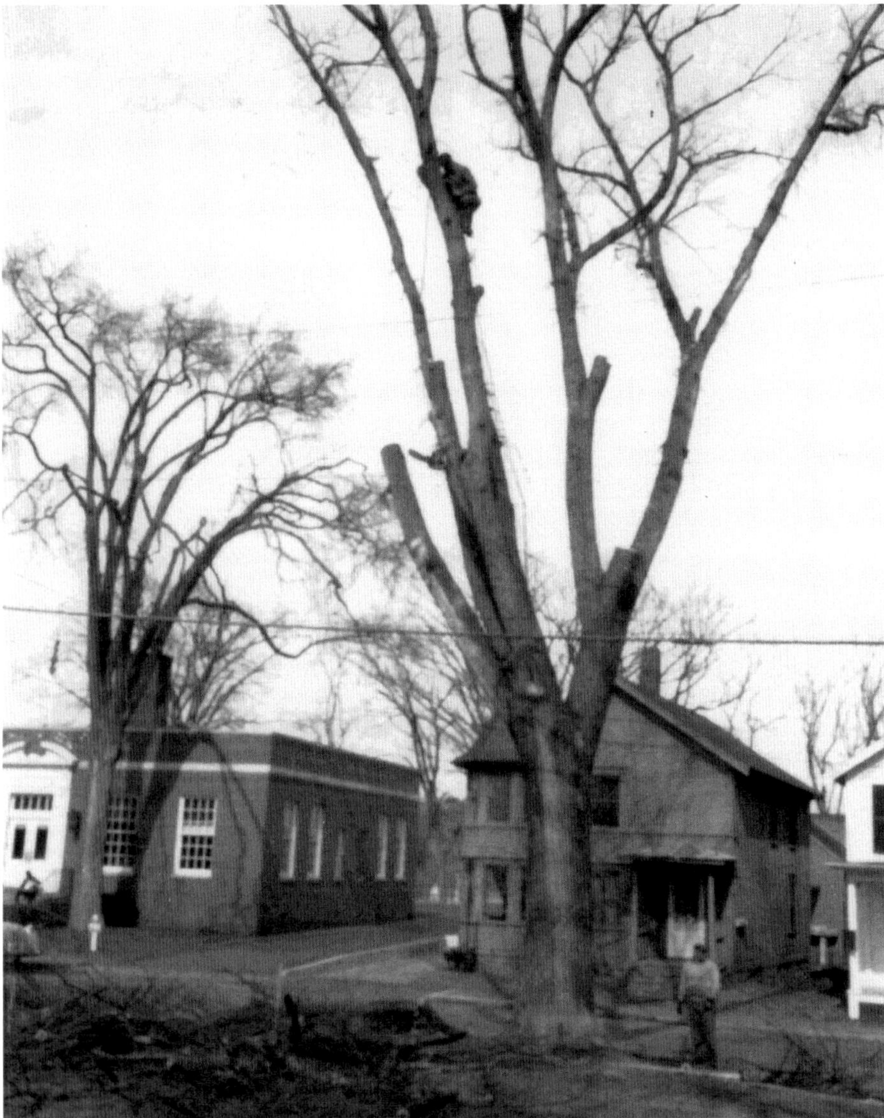

Two diseased Dutch elm trees are removed from in front of a house on Main Street in Meredith. *Courtesy of Meredith Historical Society.*

By the mid-1960s, more of Meredith's elms had died and were removed, mostly those along Scenic Park by Meredith Bay. Suddenly, the park wasn't so scenic. The lovely look of tree-lined streets in Meredith was all but gone, and there were still more trees that needed to be cut down. Archer Scribner, town manager at the time, was expecting an article pertaining to the idea of planting trees throughout the town to be discussed at town meeting in March 1965. The issue was discussed, but no immediate action was taken.

That year was a busy one. Funspot's Bob Lawton announced his run for selectman in Meredith just as Vernal "Big Buck" Bucklin was appointed second assistant chief of the Meredith Fire Department after having been a member of the department since 1936. Bob Valliere announced that he planned on closing Bob's Texaco on Main Street during the summer of the following year. In addition to running a successful gas station, the businessman was an important member of the community, as was detailed in the *Meredith News*:

> *Fellow businessmen of the Main Street area and many friends dropped in at Bob's Texaco Station Saturday at 6 p.m., the final closing hour of the business, to extend best wishes for the future to Bob Valliere.*
>
> *During his ten years as a Main Street businessman, Bob has gathered hosts of friends. His many civic activities include serving on the Planning Board, and he is currently a member of the Parks and Recreation Playgrounds*

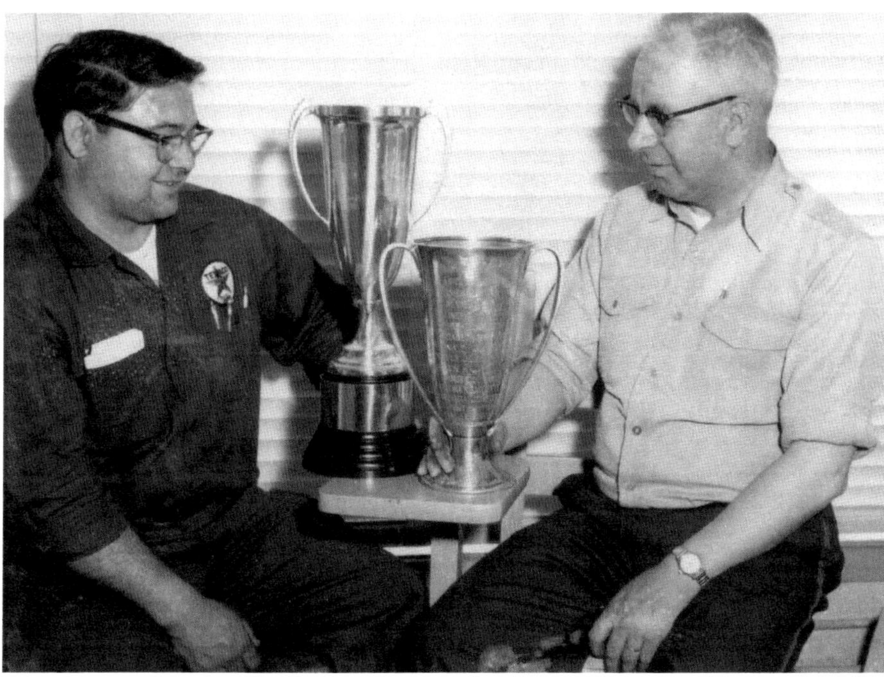

Bob Valliere (left) sits with Brad Sprague. Both men appeared many times in *Archie*. *Courtesy of Meredith Historical Society.*

> *Committee. He helped organize the Meredith Softball League 12 years ago and has continued active participation in the group. He has served as chairman of the Board of Governors of the Meredith Civic Association, was a charter member and served as president for several terms of the Meredith Lions Club and as chairman of the local Democrat Committee.*[52]

With the closure of Bob's Texaco and the heavy loss of trees along Main Street, Meredith Village looked barren and war-torn. In May 1967, it was announced that Meredith would embark on a tree-planting program, adding one hundred trees throughout the town during the spring. That signaled the beginning of a transformation of Main Street and one that Bob Montana would be involved in as he worked toward helping the town regain its charming appearance. As he did, he would also be adding one more thing to his long list of accomplishments.

Chapter 13

Artists of Distinction

During the time we lived in England, my wife and I got started on collecting art, and this led to our starting an art gallery.
—*Bob Montana,* Cartoonist PROfiles

In the beginning of 1967, Main Street in Meredith had a new look. Bob and Peg, likewise, had a new venture. They were preparing to open their own art gallery on Main Street. The idea became fully hatched during their trip to Mexico, and shortly after their return, they purchased the building that would house the future business. During their trips through the United States as well as abroad, they collected art with the thought of someday filling their own gallery and promoting art in Meredith. Peter Hall, a gifted artist and local art teacher, had already opened the Peter Hall Studio on Main Street. Once the Montanas opened the Village Gallery, Meredith had its own art colony, and it quickly became a place of culture and excitement.

Bob admitted that for him, having his own art gallery had been a lifelong dream. He was a cartoonist, but he had been trained in fine art and possessed a great love for it. In an interview for *Cartoonist PROfiles*, Bob described the path to opening his own gallery:

> *We bought a building that used to house a gas station a couple of years ago and fixed it up. If you lift the rug in one of the gallery rooms, you'll see how we covered up the old oil pit. In addition to shows of various artists' work, we have art classes, and this year, we have three teachers. Also, we started*

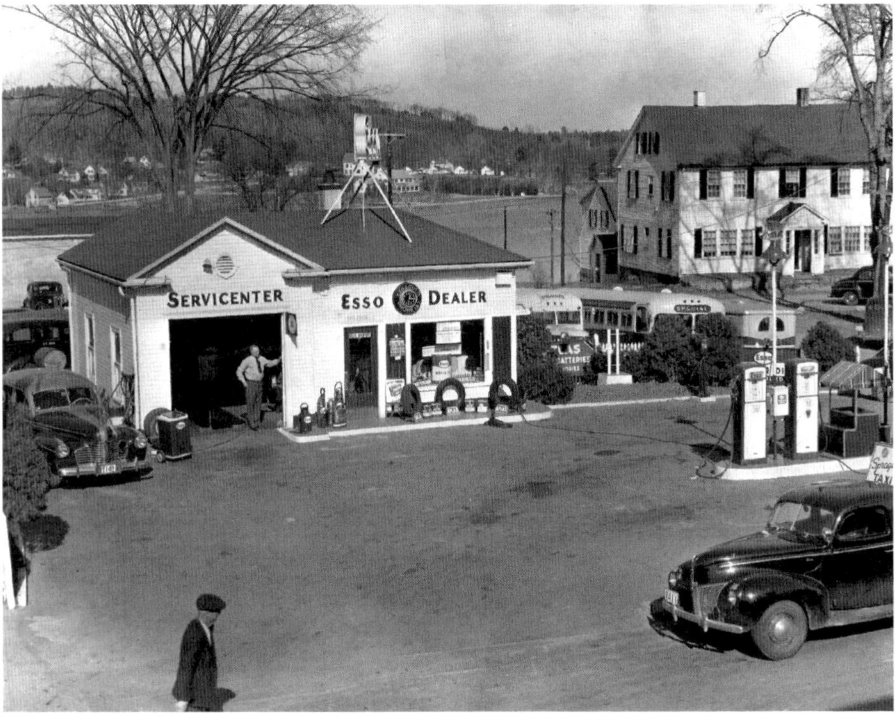

Sprague's Esso Station before it was purchased by the Montanas and transformed into an art gallery. *Courtesy of Meredith Historical Society.*

> *a framing department and found that this aspect of the gallery ran away with the whole operation.*[53]

The gas station that Bob referred to during the interview was the former Sprague Esso Service Station, which had appeared numerous times in the comic strip as Sprigs. Working with Meredith's own architect, Ralph Flather, the Montanas remodeled the old station inside and out. Alterations were made, and small extensions were added with the help of local contractor Ken Taylor.

Work on the interior décor was closely supervised by Peg and described as a wonderful blend of Early American, Williamsburg and New Hampshire farm barn. Weathered boards from an old barn in Dover, New Hampshire, were transported to Meredith by Bob and friend Elliot Bartlett. The boards' lifetime had been extended indefinitely, as they were reused as wood paneling for the sales office. The gallery was a full-service artist's paradise, as art supplies were offered for sale and a custom frame shop was housed within its walls.

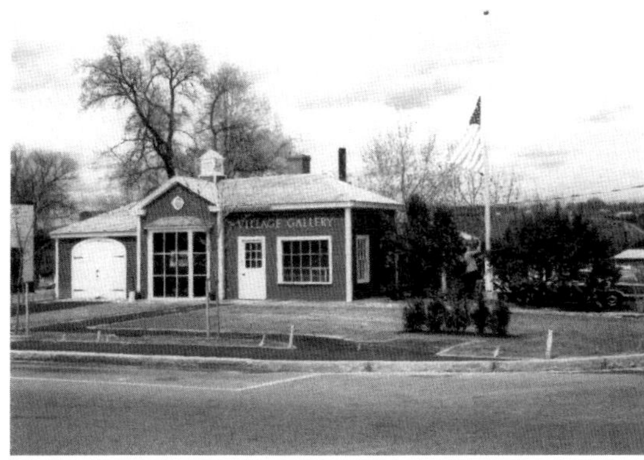

Bob raising the flag at his newly opened Village Gallery in 1967. © *Montana family*.

On opening day, the *Meredith News* ran two full pages of ads placed by local merchants saluting the Montanas' new gallery. An open house was held that included the unveiling of the first exhibit. It included paintings by artists of the nineteenth and twentieth centuries, such as Frank Moss Bennett, Atkinson Grimshaw, Henry Gillard Glindoni, Alex Mortimer and Guido Reni. Additional exhibits included the Age of English Watercolors, William Hogarth's Etchings, To the Sea in Ships, Cavalcade of Comics, Maine Oils and Watercolors by Jim Hughes, Art of the Far East, the works of David C. Baker, Dick Brooks and even some of Bob's own sketches and paintings.[54]

The opening of the Montana and Hall galleries opened up the world of art to residents of the Lakes Region, and Meredith's art colony started to blossom. Bob later commented on its development:

> *After we opened the gallery, we discovered that there were a lot of creative people around and that something like seven professional artists lived in town. Within a year, two more galleries opened up. These developments led us to the idea of trying to build an art colony in Meredith. As you know, we live on a 60-acre farm here, and we lead an easygoing type of life around our house. So, gradually we've formed the custom of having various creative people—songwriters, musicians, poets, artists, etc.—come and stay with us for perhaps a week or so at a time. Our place has sort of become the focal point for get-togethers of these people. By the way, my children—two girls and two boys ranging in ages from 20 down to 8—have told us that they enjoy being at home more than they do going somewhere else.*[55]

In July 1968, artist and musician Paul Miller set up his gallery on the corner of Main and Water Streets in Meredith. Paul was well known for his landscapes and portraiture in a variety of mediums, both in the United States and Europe. The plans he had for his gallery included having other artists come to Meredith during the summers to offer demonstrations of various media.

In his own words, Paul reflected on his journey to Meredith, the creation of his own gallery and his friendship with Bob:

> *Because I grew up in New Hampshire around the beautiful lakes, I knew that this area was a magnet for vacationers from Boston, New York and many parts of the world. I decided to look into opening a summer art gallery, and after some investigation, I discovered that a few artists were starting an art colony in Meredith, New Hampshire. An artist by the name of Peter Hall was the first gallery established, and then Bob Montana built a beautiful gallery where he had art collected from many parts of the world. I decided I wanted to be part of this effort, and I found a great location on Main Street in Meredith and signed a lease.*
>
> *During this period, I got to know Bob very well, and over the following years, we became good friends. I had good success during the first summer. During the following years, I painted during the winter months in Boston and played music with many musicians in and around the Berklee College of Music. This is where I met my great friend Steve Hulse. He and I would visit Bob and his family on Meredith Neck Road during the winter and summer months, and they always made us feel like part of their family.*
>
> *I got to see the reality of how Bob produced his* Archie *strip. He had to be a number of weeks ahead at all times, and because he needed new material constantly, he drew from his everyday experiences. He dealt in what he called "gags," which are short-story setups followed by a punch line. Some were based on tongue-in-cheek humor found in real-life situations—pulling friends from his life, renaming them and including them in a particular strip. Bob used to call me "Bunky." I played bass, so before too long, I became "Bunky the Bass Player." In 1970, he included me in one of his strips.*[56]

Paul's musician friends were finding their way to Meredith, and one of them was Steve Hulse, a pianist. While Paul Miller had been dubbed "Bunky," Bob gave Steve the nickname "Schultz." He described how his friendship with Bob and Peg began and then flourished:

> *I met Bob around 1967 at his framing shop in Meredith. My friend and roommate at the time, Paul Miller, had known Bob for a while, as Paul was an accomplished watercolor painter. Paul and I had drinks at the farm*

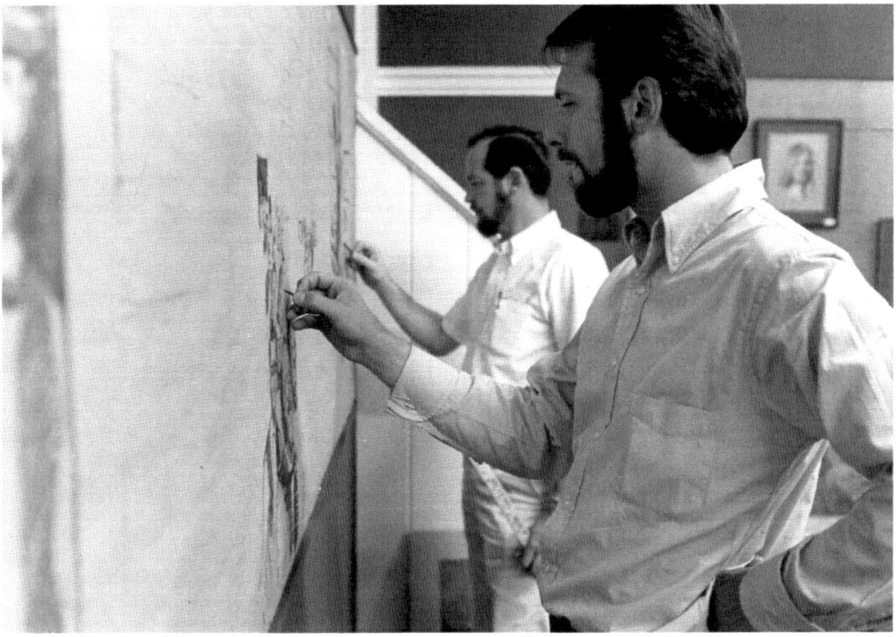

Artists Paul Miller and Bob Montana drawing a twenty-four-foot mural used in Meredith's bicentennial film. © *Montana family*.

with the family several times, then got invited to dinner, then were invited to work on his film about Meredith's history with him, and I slowly became a friend of the family. From time to time, I would drive up from Boston for a long weekend with them. They would feed me, put me up in the spare room and treat me like family.

She [Peg] *was the matron of the house. She was always calm, cool and collected...she cooked and kept the house clean and always made it look effortless. Her demeanor was always warm and open, and she was a large reason that I always felt so welcome there. My favorite memory of her was sitting in Bob's study after the dinner dishes were put away, sewing or knitting in a rocking chair next to the lamp, either listening to us talking about music or whatever, or just being with us listening to music or watching TV, which we rarely did in that house. There were always other, more interesting things going on there.*

I spent my first Christmas away from home with the Montana family. It was soft, wintry and wonderful, as one would expect. We exchanged gifts and enjoyed Christmas music and each other's company. My mom was most upset with me for not coming home, and she wasn't sure if this "Montana

> *family of Archie Comics" was real or a fabrication of mine to stay in the East for the holidays. The next spring, Mom and Dad made the trip back to Boston to visit me and nearly demanded to drive up to New Hampshire and meet these "Montanas." Bob and Peg were gracious and friendly as always, and my folks came away from that afternoon with a different view of the kinds of friends I was making "back East."*[57]

The Montana home was indeed a gathering place for talented artists and musicians. Anyone who visited or stayed there came away from that farmhouse with warm memories. Steve Hulse recalled one particular evening that he shared with Bob and his friend Paul Miller:

> *Bob loved music—pretty music, orchestral music. He liked some jazz, but it had to be the watered-down variety. He loved playing drums with Paul playing bass and me playing the little spinet in their living room. I know he loved that. He was fascinated that Paul and I loved jazz the way we did and were getting pretty decent at playing at what he considered to be a young age (Paul and I were around twenty-six to twenty-nine at the time, I think).*
>
> *I remember one evening we were sitting in his study with Peg, talking about something, and Bob had some radio jazz going on in the background. When a particular song ended, it ended with a jazzy sort of atonal chord. Bob screwed up his face a little and then grinned. He said in his quiet voice to Paul and me, "Why do they have to end those tunes with those strange chords? Why can't they just use a nice major chord that's more pleasing and call it good?"*
>
> *I had always liked those jazzy, offshoot ending chords, and not liking to go against anything Bob thought, I didn't know what to say. Then Paul said, "Oh, I like those kinds of ending chords. I think they're cool. And besides, they're different than what most music does, and I like that, too."*
>
> *Well, Bob thought that was a perfectly reasonable explanation, but it didn't change his mind about liking most jazz endings. From that evening on, whenever we played together, we always ended with a pleasant major chord and a wink. I loved those times and felt like I was part of a truly wonderful, loving family. And in fact, I was for a time.*[58]

Bob and Peg Montana may have added much to the lives of those around them, but they did the same for the town of Meredith. When they remodeled the old Esso station into a gallery, they also landscaped the grounds surrounding it. It was then that Bob put into action the plan he had to help restore the tree-lined sides of Main Street. He planted two sugar maple saplings in front of his art gallery, a few feet back from the sidewalk. He then talked with the abutting property owners and convinced each of them to plant two trees in the front of their establishments. In his own quiet way, he helped Main Street recover from the devastation caused by the loss of its trees and from its required expansion.

Chapter 14

Two Hundred Years and Counting

I was always very fond of Bob…he was a great friend to Meredith.
—Bill Allen, son of Jesse Allen, proprietor of Allen Barber Shop

Bob and Peg Montana were great friends to the town of Meredith, and as the Montana children grew older, they followed along in their parents' footsteps. Helping the community became a family mission, and the Montanas did it with flair.

While the old Esso station was transformed into the Village Gallery, a new group formed in Meredith. In 1966, two years before Meredith's bicentennial, a special committee was created, and its members spent two years planning one of the biggest celebrations Meredith had ever experienced. The first item on the committee's agenda was to set the dates of the celebration, which members chose as the week of July 27 through August 4, 1968.

Some of the town's most illustrious residents, including Brad Sprague, Will Grad and John Sherman, met to sift through their ideas and suggestions. Bob Valliere suggested that a small book on the history of Meredith be written. Bob Montana had his heart set on creating a film to commemorate one of the town's most notable birthdays. Offering its full support, the committee had already begun to discuss the idea for a movie with him. After the release of his highly acclaimed film, *The Close Shave*, no one doubted that Bob would do an outstanding job on a bicentennial movie.

In March 1968, the committee called for applications from individuals interested in becoming contestants in the Meredith Bicentennial Queen

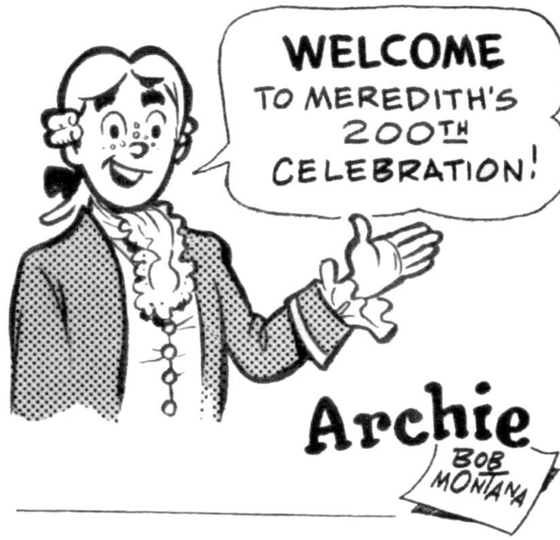

Archie welcomed all to Meredith's bicentennial celebration. © *Montana family*.

Pageant. In May, nineteen-year-old Paige Montana became one of the earliest contenders to sign up for the contest scheduled for the first day of June. In total, nine contestants entered, all vying for a long list of valuable prizes, along with the opportunity to reign over all events that were part of the bicentennial. During the competition, the girls were judged on three elements: personality, poise and beauty. Competition was fierce, but when the winner was announced, it was Paige who was crowned Miss Meredith Bicentennial. Her summer schedule was full of activity as she represented Meredith during various events, including the role of judge for the popular beard-growing contest.

While Paige was focused on her duties, Bob worked on his film, which would be titled *Meredith: The First 200 Years*. The movie was based on stories about Meredith's colorful history, written for the occasion by locals Agnes Pickering, Solon Colby and Carl Colby. Photographer Chet Brickett, artist Paul Miller and musician Shep Spinney spent long hours filming with Bob to ensure that the movie would be finished in time for the end of July.

Chet Brickett was one of the artists that came to live and work within Meredith's art colony and was self-employed as a freelance photographer. He rightfully earned the designation of official bicentennial photographer, as he was considered one of the most outstanding photographers in the region. Chet's professional background included fourteen years in Los Angeles spent working in theatrical portraiture, stage production, movies, commercials and publicity. The wide scope of his expertise made him invaluable during the production of the movie.

Paul Miller worked side by side with Bob, and together they created a twenty-four-foot mural that was scanned by the cameras when it was finished. The drawing helped to illustrate the story of what is known in

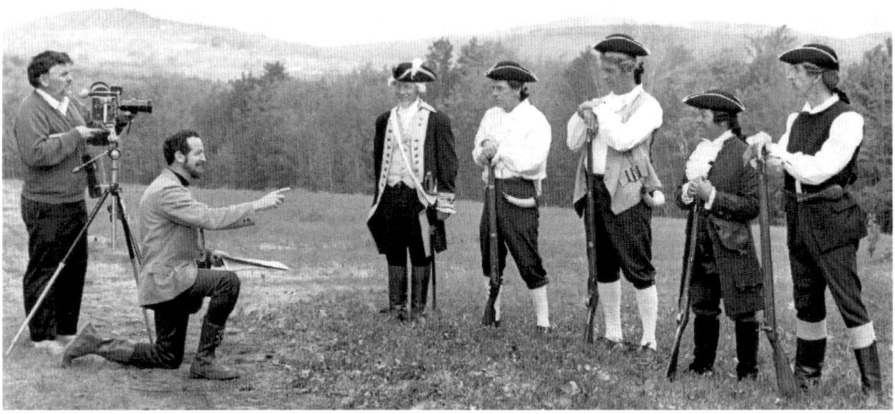

Chet Brickett, Bob Montana (directing), Gordon Grad, Linden Grad, Syne Batchelder, Ray Roux and Dick Guion taping *The First 200 Years*. *© Montana family*.

Meredith as the Great Catastrophe. In 1855, a catastrophic collapse of the floor occurred in Meredith's new town hall during a town meeting. Out of the nearly six hundred individuals who attended the meeting, at least four men were killed, many died a short time afterward, over sixty were seriously injured and others were maimed for life. Medical help was called in from as far away as Concord, New Hampshire, and the community struggled for decades to overcome the effects of the tragedy.[59]

With various aspects of the town's history chosen to be represented in the film, Bob recruited residents to become actors in the movie. Vernal Bucklin, Ernie Lavalle, Linden and Will Grad, Ray Roux, C. Paul Reed and Dick Guion led the cast of stars. Friends Jean Allen, Marge Bacon and Ruth Harding had small but exciting roles. Even Bob's youngest son, Don, became a cast member, and in order for his appearance to be historically accurate, he grew out his hair.

The weather proved to be a constant challenge during the filming, as the project was plagued with one rainstorm after another. Actors stood by, ready to jump in when the sun finally poked out from behind the clouds. Bob and his crew spent numerous late-night sessions toiling over the film; one work session lasted until almost five o'clock in the morning. Chet reported that over three thousand feet of film had been shot, with more being used on a daily basis. After shooting the film, sound and any special effects were added in, which increased the time the crew spent editing.

When it came to a celebration as large as the town's bicentennial, Bob was not content to stop at just the contribution of a movie. He helped create the program cover of the bicentennial program, and his drawing from the program appeared on the First Day Issue for the Meredith bicentennial. During the summer, Bob and Peg opened their historic 1770s farmhouse during a public tour of the oldest and finest homes in town. In July, an *Archie* strip showed Archie's mother, Mrs. Andrews, purchasing a wig for the Bicentennial Ball.

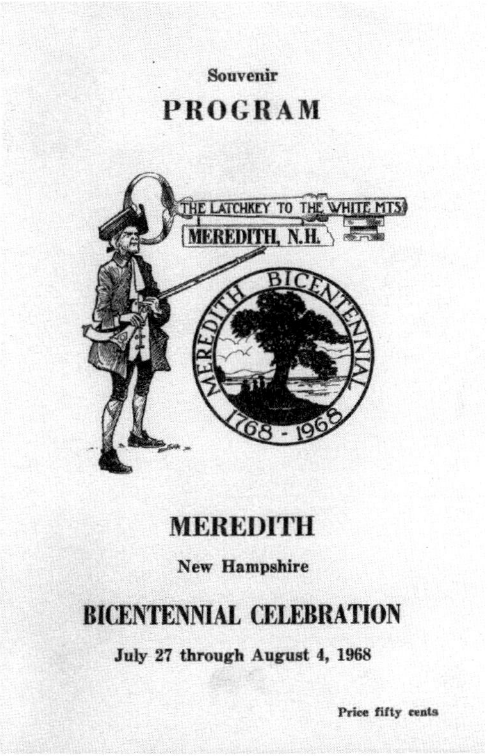

Meredith's 1968 bicentennial program cover featured Bob's illustration. © *Montana family*.

The Montanas called upon their friends in the world of comics to contribute to an impressive cartoon auction that was held in conjunction with a coin auction. The event was held on the lawn of the town's library, and the goal was to have a portion of the proceeds from the event go directly to the library for the purchase of art and art reference books.

Bob's fellow cartoonists were solicited for pieces of original work, and he gathered a large amount of work drawn by some of America's top cartoonists. An original *Archie* strip topped the list, along with *Peanuts* by Charles Schultz, *Beetle Bailey* by Mort Walker, *Little People* by Walt Scott, *Short Ribs* by Frank O'Neal, Bill Holman's *Smokey Stover* and *Andy Capp* by Reg Smythe, England's leading cartoonist. The comic strips were on exhibit at the Village Gallery, which was opened to the public one week prior to the auction. The unique fundraising event was later billed as one of the highlights of the entire bicentennial celebration.

On July 27, 1968, the official bicentennial celebration got underway with the reading of a proclamation by Selectman Robert Rhodes as the Meredith Militiamen of '68 fired a musket volley on the lawn of the

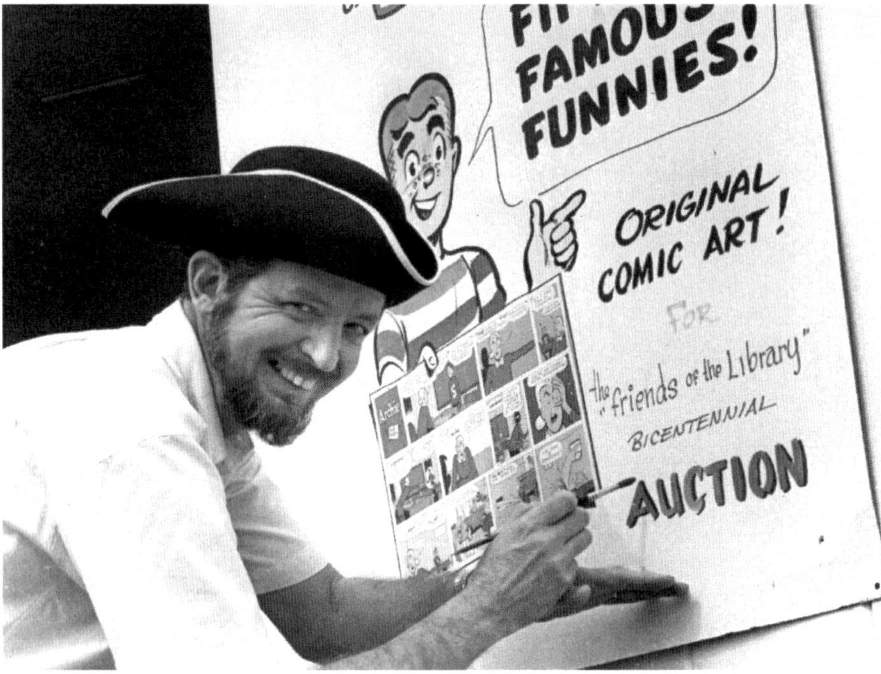

Bob works to finish a sign advertising a comic auction at Meredith Public Library. © *Montana family*.

Village Gallery. Following the opening ceremony, a large parade running the length of Main Street showcased numerous floats, all of which had been painstakingly constructed and decorated. In her role as Bicentennial Queen, Paige was seen during the parade waving from a convertible covered with delicate pink and white flowers. The entire Montana family dressed in period costumes, and Bob's movie had been completed in time for the first day of festivities.

Meredith residents worked relentlessly to make the town's bicentennial an enjoyable and memorable one. The work of the bicentennial committee continued after the celebration, and Paige carried on with her commitment as queen. In the middle of July 1969, two time capsules were buried side by side in the library lawn. One was scheduled to be opened fifty years from the bicentennial, in 2018, and the other during the 300th anniversary of the town in 2068. The capsules include an *Archie* comic strip and a letter from Bicentennial Queen Paige Montana to the Tercentennial Queen.

During the ceremony, Stewart Lamprey, then co-chair of the New England Regional Commission, spoke and emphasized the need for residents to

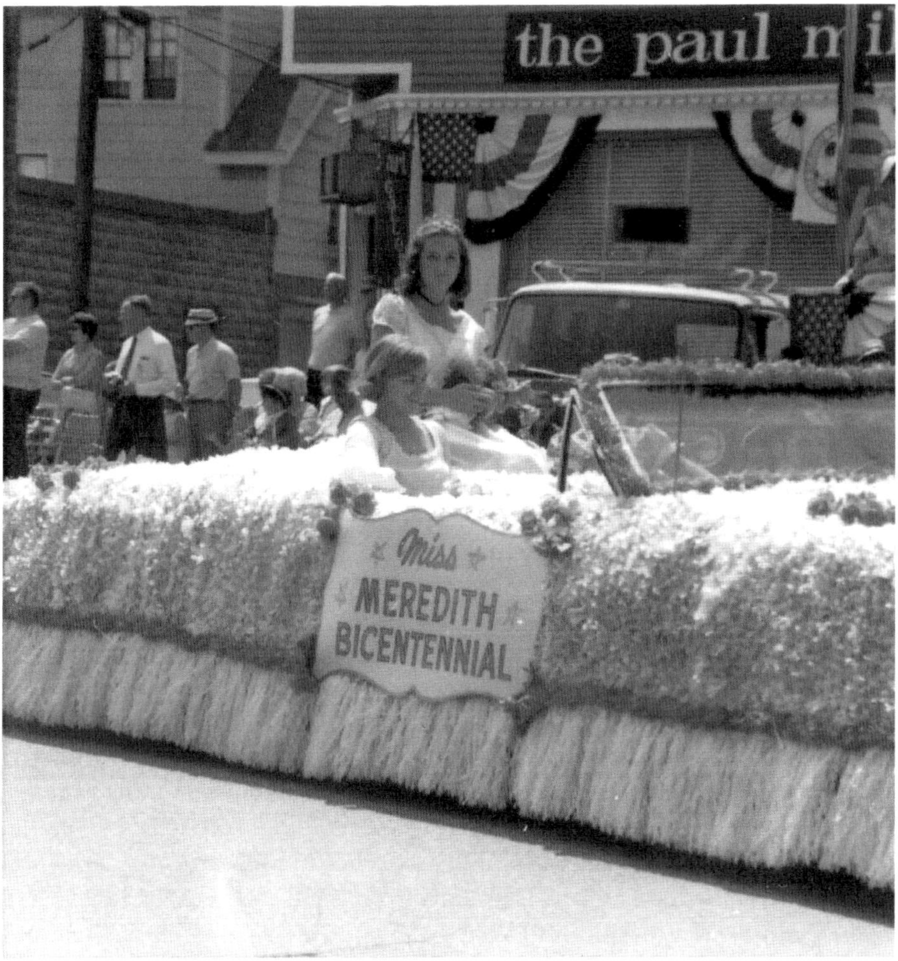

Paige Montana, Meredith's Bicentennial Queen, in the parade along Main Street. The Paul Miller Gallery serves as a backdrop. *Courtesy of the Meredith Historical Society.*

continually strive to retain the magnificence of New Hampshire. As the time capsules were lowered into their long-term home, the Meredith Militia blasted off a volley as the marble lid was lowered into place. Peg Montana presented to the library a volume that summarized the events of the bicentennial both in photographs and words. Bob stood by her side and then presented a copy of the bicentennial film for the library's archives.[60]

The commitment of Meredith to its bicentennial caught the attention of some important individuals. In December 1974, the town received the honor of being named one of the nation's Bicentennial Communities, one

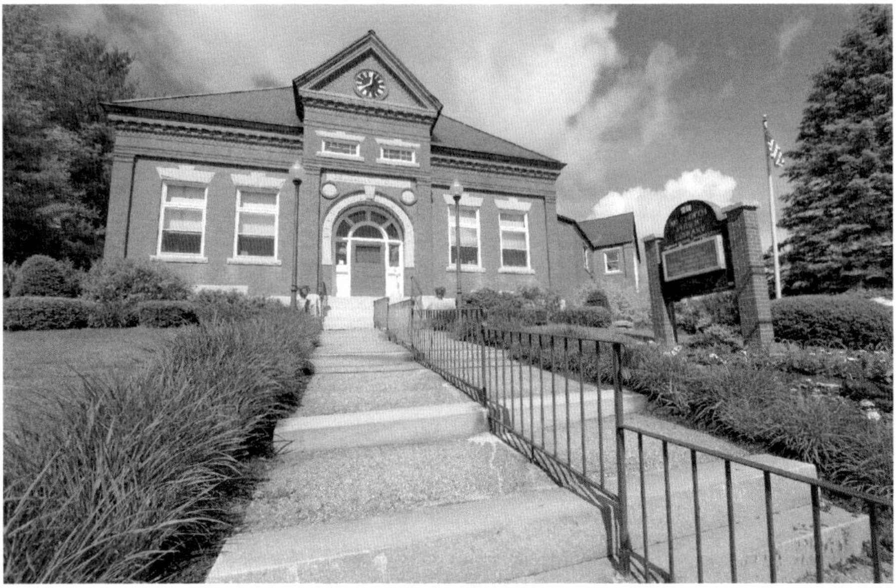

Meredith Public Library on Main Street. Bob was a great supporter of the library and its activities. *Photo by Harrison Haas.*

of fifteen in the state and one of two thousand in the nation. The town was so honored by the National American Revolution Bicentennial Administration, the organization in charge of coordinating the nation's bicentennial.

In a letter received by the regional coordinator of the organization, the town was notified that the community had been designated a National Bicentennial Community. The recognition had been extended to the municipality because of the fine bicentennial program planned by the Meredith bicentennial committee. The group was required to complete one project of lasting significance in the community, and committee members had already been authorized by the town selectmen to commence the development of the John Bond Swasey Park on Lake Waukewan.[61]

It did not matter whether the people of Meredith organized their bicentennial celebration or events connected to the national event, they could be counted on to do an outstanding job. With its own bicentennial behind them, residents looked forward to America's 200th anniversary celebration. However, no matter how much Bob wanted to be involved in the nation's birthday, he would not play a part in any of the activities held during the nation's bicentennial in 1976.

Chapter 15

Ask a Busy Person

The 1970 New Hampshire Easter Seal Appeal has broken the state record for the third successive year—by almost $20,000, Campaign Chairman Bob Montana of Meredith announced today.

—Meredith News, *June 1970*

Benjamin Franklin once said, "If you want something done, ask a busy person." Mr. Franklin's philosophical statement was custom-made for a person like Bob Montana. The relentless, unforgiving deadlines Bob faced each week caused his schedule to be heavily laden with pressure, yet it never stopped him from finding the time to support those who asked for his help. Charity work was done over and above everything else on his personal agenda, and the assistance he offered was carefully woven into a full life. Bob knew that his celebrity status could provide an enormous boost to fundraising efforts, and in some cases, simply his endorsement of a good cause made the biggest difference.

After his discharge from the army in 1946, and throughout his adult life, Bob took an active role in overseas USO tours.[62] He was a favorite due not only to the fact that he could he draw Archie but also because his vaudeville training enabled him to tell jokes and entertain. In order to not have to deal with the creation of comic strips while on the road, he made sure that *Archie* was fourteen weeks ahead of schedule. For several weeks before his departure, twelve-hour workdays were not uncommon in order to accomplish this goal.

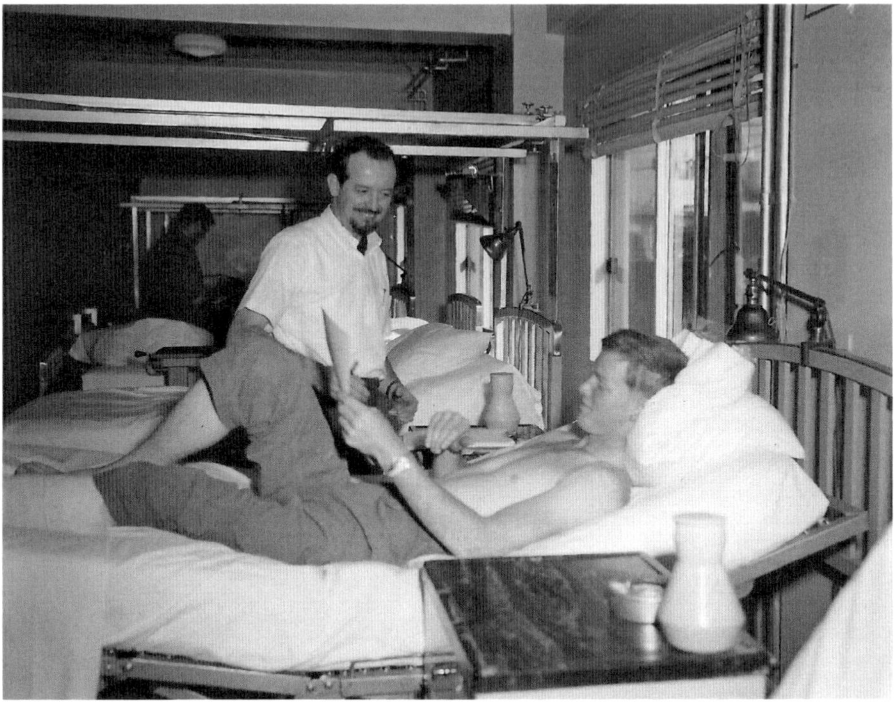

Bringing a few laughs to wounded and homesick American soldiers during USO trips was something Bob did quite often. © *Montana family*.

At the beginning of October 1952, Bob was off to Europe for a five-week USO tour of American bases in Europe. He made the trip with nine other members of the National Cartoonists Society, flying first to Cambridge, England. From there, they visited camps in North Africa, Germany and France. As was customary, his Jazzstick was his constant companion on all tours, and he played it during every show. Bob would often tease the soldiers that they could make a replica of his Jazzstick by "finding an MP with a billy and then throwing the MP away."[63]

Upon his return from the tour, Bob told a reporter for the *Meredith News* that the group had given thirty shows in twenty-two camps. He further explained how the cartoonists performed on stages as elaborate as the theater with a $1 million chandelier in Wiesbaden, Germany, to a plank of wood in a stable in France. Their goal was to entertain the troops, and they did it with style—in mess halls, hospital wards and outside under blue skies. Bob was delighted to report that out of the thirty-eight different comic books read by the troops, *Archie* was the third most popular.[64]

A few years later, in a March 28, 1955 letter to Bob from U.S. Air Force Colonel Joseph Goetz, the gratitude the military had for the willingness of Bob and his fellow cartoonists to visit soldiers was apparent:

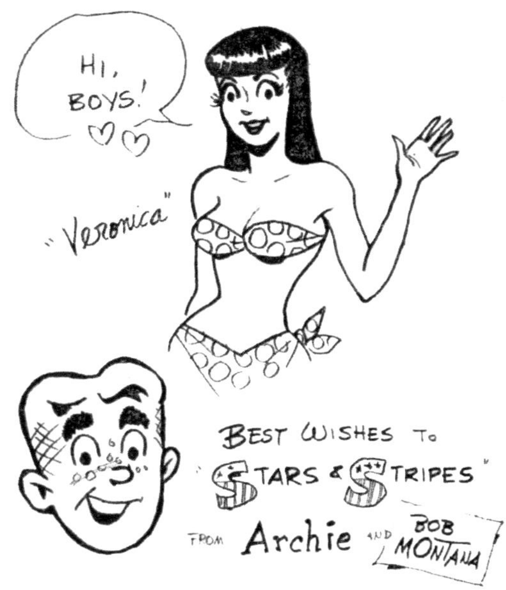

A typical Archie-and-Veronica drawing Bob created during USO trips. © *Montana family*.

> *Accept our sincerest thanks for your graciousness and generosity of personal time and effort devoted to the two-day Dayton trip last March 17th and 18th. Indeed, they are still talking about it out there, especially the poor devils in the hospital. Colonel Jim Crehan informed me in a telephone conversation that the Red Cross folks told him you cartoonists were positively the most encouraging and entertaining group to visit the hospital.*
>
> *As for me, I know what you went through in that rough ride from New York to Dayton—and without a complaint—to put on a show practically minutes after you landed. So accept my personal thanks and gratitude.*

In 1956, one day after Christmas, Bob was included in a talented collection of artists and musicians that left for Egypt from New York. It was the first group sent to that country to entertain the troops of the United Nations. The trip was sponsored by the United Nations, which was working directly with the Overseas Entertainment Committee of the National Cartoonists Society. Al Posen, creator of *Sweeney and Son*, acted as chairman of the committee, which included *Esquire* magazine artist E. Simms Campbell and musicians from Duke Ellington's band.

On the way back to the States, the entertainers stopped in Rome to celebrate New Year's Eve and then headed to New York City the next day. Peg, her parents and the Montana children were at the airport to greet Bob upon his arrival back home. They all then made the trip back to Meredith to resume their own interrupted holiday celebrations.

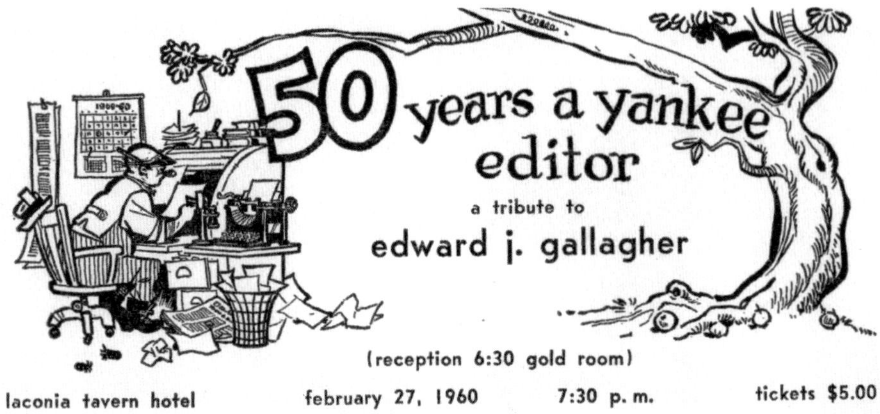

Bob organized a 1960 tribute to Ed Gallagher, publisher and editor of the *Laconia Evening Citizen*. © *Montana family*.

Early in 1960, Bob was involved in something closer to home. He sent out personal letters to scores of friends, inviting them to a tribute for Edward J. Gallagher. Edward was editor and publisher of the *Laconia Evening Citizen*, a well-respected newspaper in the Lakes Region. The event, called "50 Years a Yankee Editor," was masterminded and organized by Bob. In his letter about the tribute, Bob wrote, "On February 27, 1960, several hundred newspapermen and celebrities will gather to honor Mr. Edward J. Gallagher. The love and respect this man has won in over fifty years of publishing typifies the great heritage of the Newspaper Industry."[65]

Gather they did. The event was attended by newspapermen and well-known personalities from throughout New England. Bob received high praise for his dedication and hard work, which included a series of cartoons he created that illustrated the different stages of his dear friend's career.

During the summer of 1963, another local organization benefited from the popularity of Bob and his pal Archie. The cartoonist agreed to become a member of the Meredith fundraising committee of the Lakes Region Family Services Association. Each year, the organization sent out its annual appeal letters in August, with Meredith's annual quota set for at least $500. Bob created a special drawing of Archie, which was included in the organization's special letter to area residents. When the unique drawing appeared in mailboxes throughout town, Meredith's quota was easily surpassed.

A quick trip south from the Lakes Region allowed Bob to judge the Spring Arts Festival in Boston during 1968. His fellow judge, Joseph Trippetti, the executive director of the League of Arts and Crafts in Manchester, traveled with him. The two men worked together for hours as they patiently judged the large amount of work on display. Peter Hall of Meredith was an exhibitor, and his art attracted some of the largest crowds among the nearly two hundred artists taking part in the event. The talented artist won third prize in the watercolor category.

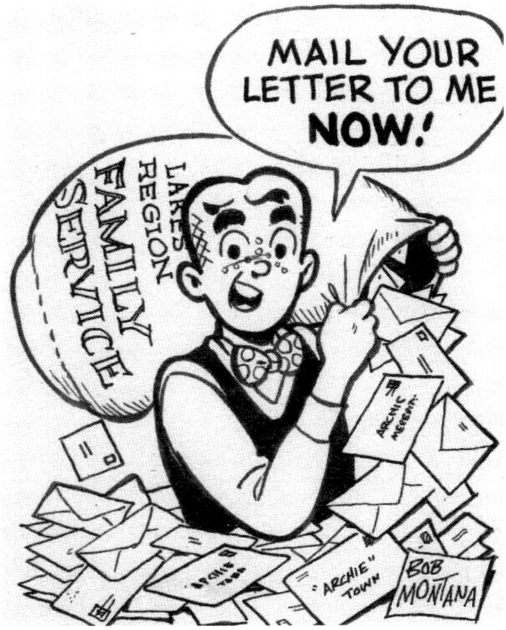

Lakes Region Family Services' fundraising efforts were helped by Bob and Archie. © *Montana family*.

Shortly after serving as judge, Bob flew to the Far East for a three-week USO tour of U.S. military hospitals there. By his side were fellow cartoonists John Sorensen, Glenn Bernhardt and Stu Moldren. Bob was the appointed head of the group of cartoonists, which was known as the Pix Pack.[66] He was interviewed by a reporter and described what the cartoonists' goal was: "What we're doing is simply walking around the wards, talking to the boys and sketching a cartoon, portrait or anything they'd like." He talked about his own army days, saying, "We had quite a crew in the barracks in those days. There were a lot of Disney artists working on army films, and we also had Sam Cobean and Charles Addams, who later went on to become famed magazine cartoonists." Bob got a big surprise at a hospital in Japan when he heard a soldier yell, "Hey, Bob! How's things in New Hampshire?"[67] He turned around and found Jimmie St. Cyr, a U.S. Marine, of Laconia.

In March 1969, one of Bob's most ambitious fundraising challenges presented itself. Archie was named the 1969 New Hampshire Easter Seals chairman, as announced by then-president Alexander M. Taft. In his statement, he said that Archie, famous star of television, newspapers and comic books, was selected as chairman because he represents "the clean-cut if somewhat confused modern teenager." He continued, "In these days of constant criticism of young people, the part played by teenagers in our annual Easter Seals campaign is most encouraging."[68]

Immediately after Alexander Taft's statement, Archie held his own press conference to tell the world that a Meredith resident by the name of Bob Montana would be his co-chairman. Bob was quick to say that he fully expected to do most of the work. Archie spoke up and said that he had already enlisted the help of his friends Jughead, Veronica, Betty, the Principal, Flutesnoot, Svenson, Miss Hagley, Mr. Lodge and Miss Grundy. Bob added that he felt the list would have to include more names if the chair and co-chair were going to achieve their goal of beating the state record of almost $68,000 that had been set during the previous year's campaign.

Bob already knew how he planned on breaking the record. Instead of the usual appeal letter, the 1969 "letter" was none other than a custom-made *Archie* comic describing the work of the Easter Seals Association. Everyone could identify with *Archie*, as the comic strip appeared in over six hundred daily newspapers and was enjoyed by over 80 million readers throughout the world. The mailing, accompanied by the *Archie* strip, was the largest in the organization's history and spread to every city and town in the state. Approximately 250,000 seals and annual appeal letters were mailed.

While the mailing worked its magic, the annual Easter Seals banquet was held. The featured speaker was the former owner of three major league baseball teams, the "incorrigible maverick" Bill Veeck.[69] He also had recently become the president of Suffolk Downs racetrack. Bob spoke during the banquet and said that having Veeck speak at the banquet would spotlight the fact that New Hampshire's Easter Seals Division was a national champion.

In the beginning of July, Bob was pleased to announce that the 1969 campaign had indeed set an all-time record totaling over $75,000, nearly a 10 percent increase over the previous year's total. He was quick to comment, saying, "On behalf of the drive workers—and especially on behalf of the disabled and handicapped who are aided by Easter Seals—I want to express our great appreciation to the 35,000 Granite State families and businesses which made this record possible."[70]

In 1970, another announcement came from the Easter Seals Association. It stated that New Hampshire's best-known teenager and an artist from the town of Meredith planned on being the chairmen of the 1970 Easter Seals annual appeal. Archie and Bob were set on breaking their own record from the previous year. In an article that appeared in the *Meredith News*, the comical duo played it up as only they could:

> *Archie pointed out that his friend Ed Sullivan is this year's national campaign chairman, his friend Carol Burnett was last year, and his friend*

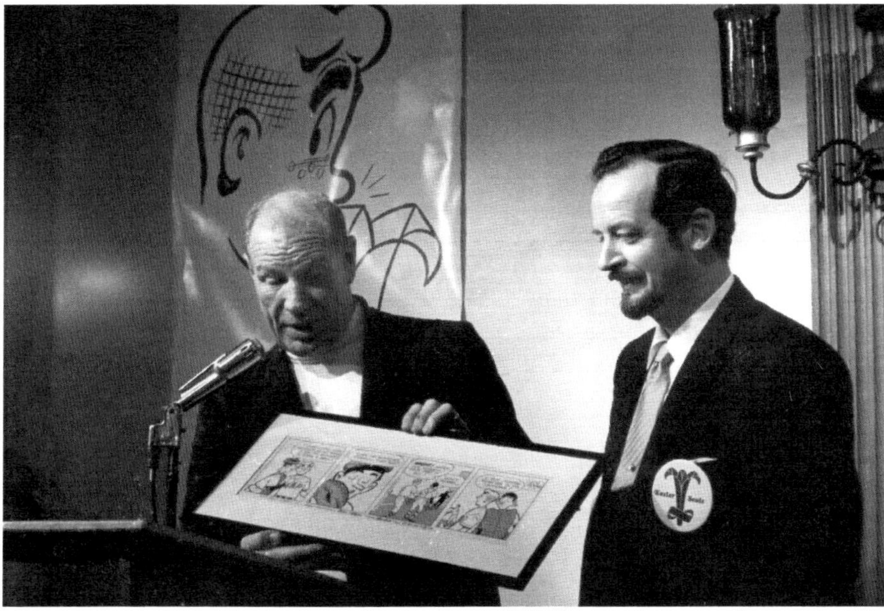

Baseball team owner Bill Veeck (left) appears with Bob during an Easter Seals banquet. © *Montana family*.

> *Dinah Shore was the year before that. "My special friend Pearl Bailey is helping Ed Sullivan this year," added Archie.*
>
> *Quoting his friend comedian Jimmy Durant, a national Easter Seal volunteer for over a quarter of a century, Archie signed off with a typical witticism: "Everybody wants ta get into da act, we hope." After Archie finished, his friend Bob Montana admonished him for not asking everyone to be sure to send in their dollars. "Send five," quipped Archie, "they're small these days."*[71]

In June, when the final fundraising figures were announced, Bob and his teenage sidekick had once again broken the state record. This time, the total amount raised was more than $20,000 over the previous year's amount. Bob made the official announcement and explained that well over $94,000 had been raised, representing a nearly 26 percent increase.

Bob and Archie certainly had the Midas touch. Even if it meant rearranging his work schedule or disrupting his family's holiday celebrations, Bob always gave of himself, and in a big way. It was never for the glory; rather, it was to help make the lives of those around him better and brighter. He was a highly respected man in many circles, but because of his selflessness, he had earned that admiration.

Chapter 16

Life's Reflections

You can't help but express your own views and ideas. Lately, I've been conscious of doing it. I hope people who read Archie *have noticed it.*
—Bob Montana, September 1969

By the time Bob reached middle age, he had attained lofty goals both personally and professionally. He had a wonderful family, *Archie* was as popular as ever and he easily maintained his position as being one of America's top cartoonists. He was well aware, however, that there was more to life than being at the top of one's game. His own feeling of success came from sources far removed from his professional life. Friend Steve Hulse was fortunate enough to have gained an intimate insight into the cartoonist's view of the relationship he had with his famous comic strip. Bob's comments could easily have surprised his friend or anyone who might have been a part of the conversation. The message in his straightforward statements was clear as he explained with a smile, "What kind of person would you take me for if my ego and self-worth were wrapped up in a comic strip? I hope you think more of me than that."[72] Bob may have lived and breathed *Archie*, but that was not where he found his sense of self.

Archie is one of the few comic strips that has traveled through the decades and gracefully changed with each one. By the 1960s, gone were the days when *Archie* was without a thoughtful message tucked in here and there. Not only were the Montana children helping Bob keep up with the latest sayings, such as "switched on" or "square," but they also kept him up to date on the fashion styles: bell-bottoms, shag haircuts and go-go boots. New inventions and changes in society, such as automated stamp machines, color television sets, cameras with automatic shutters, fondue and sit-ins, were given a mention in *Archie*. Once America entered the race to put a man on the moon, Archie and the gang constantly looked for a way to send Jughead there.

Bob's children and drawing comics kept him young. Yet he was able to view the world through the eyes of a mature man. Littering, tax burdens and the introduction of computers were some of the challenges and changes society was facing, and they, too, were brought into the strip. In his own words, Bob described his newfound goal:

> *Incidentally, the writing isn't getting any easier as the years go by. I'm not always satisfied nowadays with just a joke or a gag—I want to say something. I'm trying to make the strip more contemporary and am slyly injecting some social comment wherever I can. By the way, when I do this, I get a lot more reaction from readers. As you can imagine, I think all of us should try and make the comics more contemporary, as much as we can.*[73]

Bob had no difficulty keeping his comic strip modern. His opinion of a current issue appeared in *Archie* during August 1966, which began with Archie and Jughead heading deep into the woods to meet the wealthy Mr. Lodge. Jughead asked Archie, "What's a millionaire like Mr. Lodge doing up here in a cabin?" Archie replied, "Well, once you get everything you want, then you try to get away from it." In a 1967 strip, a satisfied Mr. Lodge again appears after a long, hectic day at work, this time positively ecstatic over making a mere six dollars after taxes.

Drawing a comic strip about teenagers made young people one of the main focuses of Bob's life, but the next generation became even more important to him as he grew older. Changes that affected them and the world in which they lived were of great concern to him. He offered his opinion of America's teenagers during an interview, saying, "I have great faith in them. They're thinking so much earlier, and they mature earlier—they'll do better than we did."[74] He was committed to giving them his attention, and it mattered not whether he had to travel a short distance or a great one to visit them. In 1966, the senior class at nearby Plymouth High School chose the comical play *Archie Andrews* as the final production of their last year in high school. When they invited Bob to be their guest of honor, he was there. After watching the show with Paige, he complimented the students' production by saying that he felt they did a wonderful job of bringing his characters to life so well.

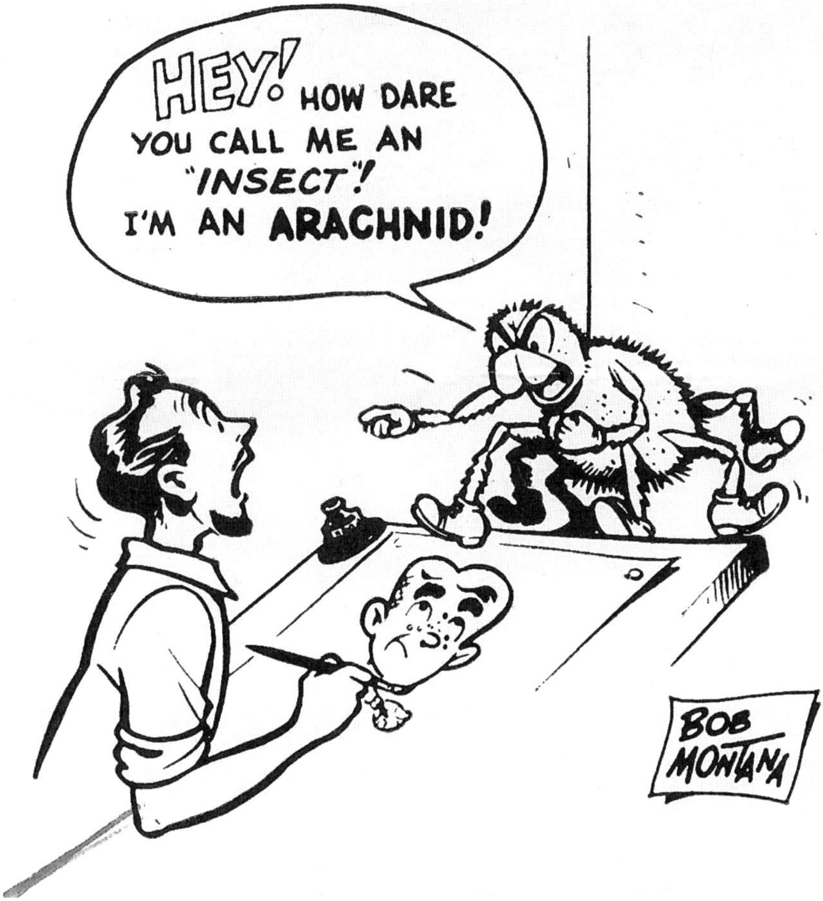

Bob created a special drawing for schoolchildren in Detroit after they pointed out that he had incorrectly labeled a spider. © *Montana family*.

Bob was one who found it easy to laugh at his own mistakes. He provided a heartwarming example of this ability after he received letters from over thirty sixth-grade students in Detroit pointing out that he had mislabeled a spider as an insect. He could have chosen to ignore the children's letters. Instead, he had fun with the situation by sending the students' teacher a note and a drawing that humorously illustrated his mistake. It appeared shortly thereafter on the front page of the *Detroit News*.

At the beginning of the fall semester in 1969, Bob traveled with five well-known cartoonists to Oklahoma State University. The highlights of his conversation with the college students were later printed in the *Daily*

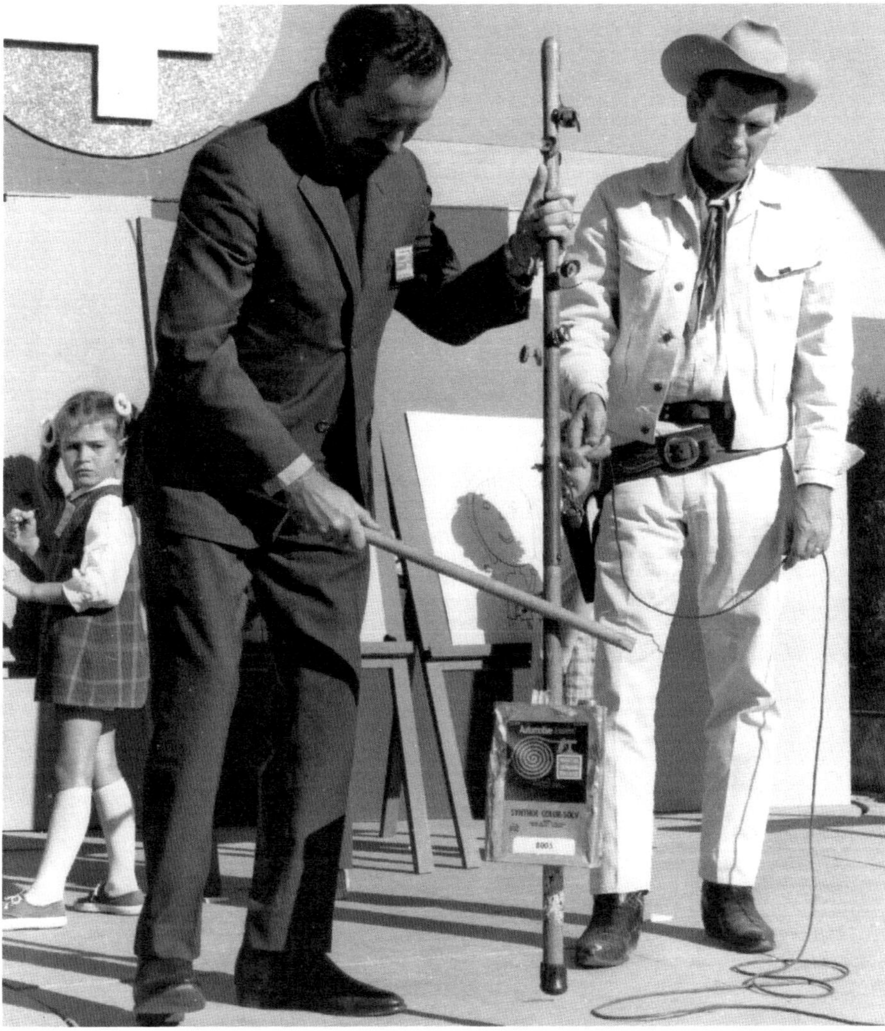

Bob playing his Jazzstick at the Oklahoma State Fair in 1969. © *Montana family*.

O'Collegian. His comments included what he envisioned for Archie's future: "Archie will never get married. That would destroy the strip." He described how he included issues that are generally criticized by the public, saying, "I try to keep hitting the establishment and air pollution." He added that one of the latest innovations in his comic strip was the introduction of a black character, an event that was newsworthy in the 1960s. He finished by offering some advice to the young journalism students:

> *Puns are the lowest form of humor, but I try to use them as part of the dialogue, not as the punch-line...I throw them in assuming everyone knows they're corny.*
>
> *Writing a daily strip means sitting down to a blank piece of paper and coming up with a situation by keeping your train of thought on it.*
>
> *It's not like a well. The more you write, the easier it is. It's when you lay off that it gets difficult.*[75]

Back home in New Hampshire, Bob became involved in larger, more complex challenges facing the community. He was especially sensitive to issues that would have a lasting negative effect on the town and its future generations. Always being one to stand up for what he believed was right, he quietly and respectfully brought about great changes in Meredith.

In 1968, a battle was waged that catapulted the town from its rural past into the present day. Meredith had no zoning regulations, and the adoption of any regulations had been voted down over a dozen times. This left its rural landscape vulnerable to developers who had an eye for commercial endeavors. In August, a disturbing announcement was made: tall, concrete condominium towers were going to be built at the head of Meredith Bay. The project was due to begin in November, and the construction of two nine-story, one-hundred-foot towers was expected to be completed by the following summer. The buildings were to be made from pre-cast concrete set on concrete columns to allow for ample parking underneath.[76]

The news sent shockwaves through the community, causing residents to immediately rally together, and Bob was among those adamantly opposed to the project. Two important meetings were scheduled in order to give residents several opportunities to discuss the height of buildings constructed in their town. The first, held in October, had an attendance of over 450 individuals. After a lengthy and spirited discussion, 209 to 35 voted in favor of limiting the height of buildings.[77]

Shortly after that meeting, residents woke up to find a huge banner hanging across one of the islands located in Meredith Bay. The banner's message was simple: "Save Our Bay." This battle went far beyond regulating the height of buildings in town; it was truly a fight to save the natural beauty of the bay and of Meredith. The identity of the individual or individuals responsible for the island banner remained a mystery. It left townspeople scratching their heads; nevertheless, it forced residents in the community to get to the heart of the matter. More importantly, it left members of Meredith's planning

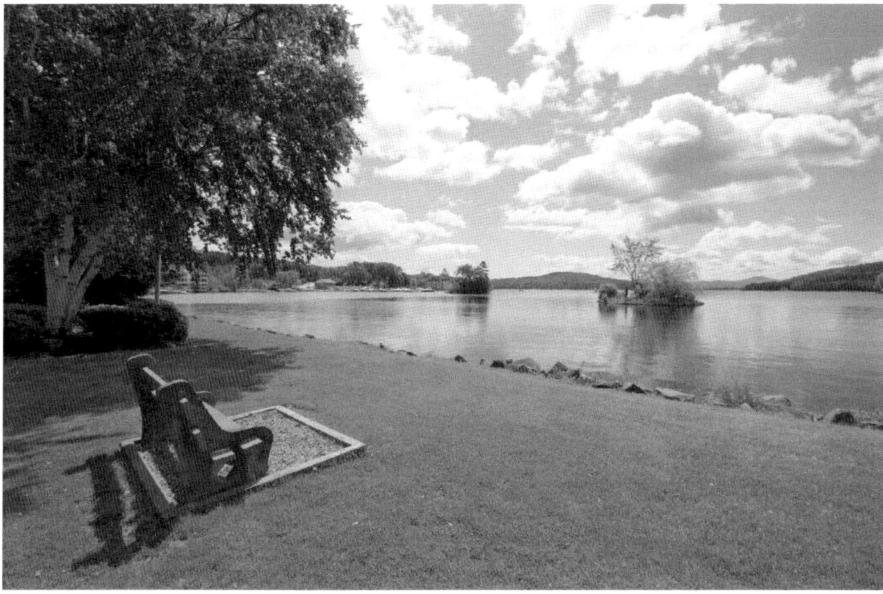

Picturesque Meredith Bay remains free of tall buildings thanks to the efforts of Bob and other Meredith residents. *Photo by Harrison Haas.*

board with no doubt that the entire town realized its lackadaisical approach to zoning was no longer good enough.

In January 1969, a public hearing was held in order for residents to learn about and review the proposed zoning ordinance, which included limiting the height of buildings, as well as the control of signs and setbacks. In April, a special town meeting was held, and with a vote of 247 to 154, new ordinances were put in place that limited the height of buildings constructed in Meredith. The proposed monstrous concrete towers were never built.[78]

A smaller challenge tackled by Bob and a handful of residents was the cumbersome parking meters along Main Street. The group banded together with the hope of convincing town officials to remove the unsightly parking meters from along the narrow sidewalks. The meters were bulky and affected the public's ability to maneuver along the store-lined street. After conducting a little research, they found that only a small amount of income came from the meters. They were subsequently removed, which left the sidewalks open to pedestrians and allowed Main Street to have a more welcoming and picturesque appearance.

The close-knit community was not all about strife, however. In January 1973, an important celebration honored two of Meredith's finest citizens, as

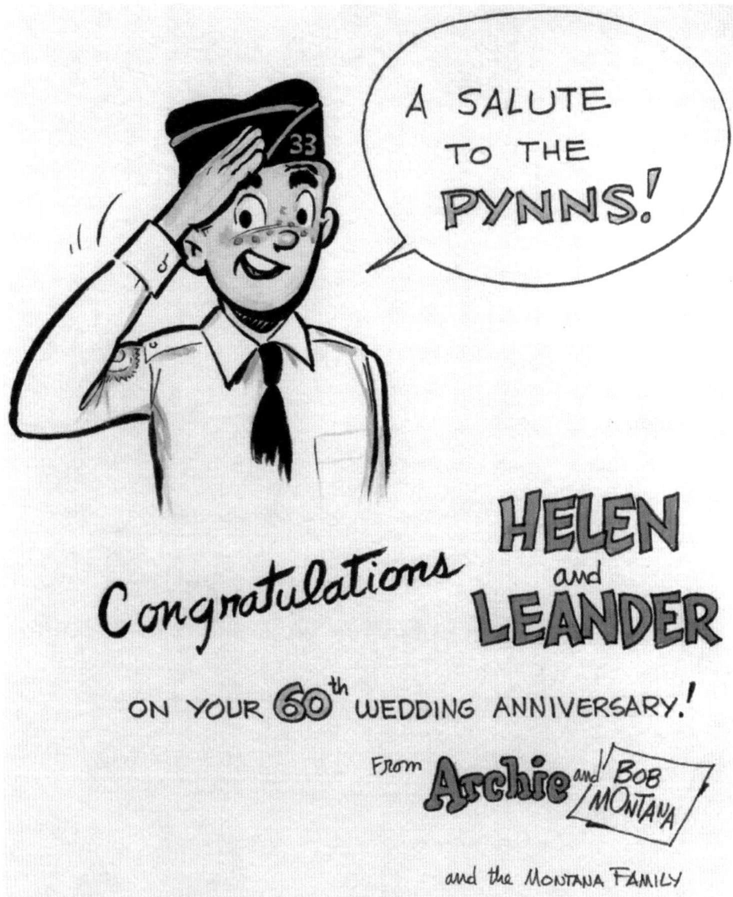

Archie helped celebrate the Pynn's sixtieth anniversary. © *Montana family*.

Helen and Leander Pynn celebrated their sixtieth wedding anniversary. The surprise party, called "one of the best-kept secrets in town," was held at the American Legion Home.[79] Friends and family arrived from across the country, and the celebration was lengthy, with the hall filled to capacity all afternoon. Attendees had one thing in mind: to thank the couple for their numerous activities from which so many had benefited. For the noteworthy occasion, Bob created a one-of-a-kind drawing of Archie that wished the Pynns a happy sixtieth anniversary.

Throughout its celebrations and struggles, Meredith continued to change in numerous ways. Family-owned businesses were sold and sometimes bought by people from outside of the Lakes Region. Grad's, founded by Sam Grad and run by clerks Linden and Willard Grad, was sold out of the family in 1964. The well-known establishment was one that was fortunate enough to survive the change of ownership and the varying trends in consumer spending. Others were not so lucky.

One of the biggest losses to old-time Meredith was that of the Weeks' Country Store in September 1973. Established in 1880, it had been a staple of Meredith's business environment for over ninety years. It underwent several name changes during the years, beginning as Green & Pease. Fred W. Weeks and a partner bought the store somewhere around 1905. In 1941, when Fred's partner died, his sons entered the business, and the store's name became F.W. Weeks & Sons. It was renamed Weeks' Country Store in 1962.

The sweeping changes in Meredith may have caused Bob some concern and additional work, but he remained focused on the next generation. Friend Bruce Heald had served one term as a selectman and ran for reelection. At the same time, he continued his work as a teacher and head of the high school music department. Exchange concerts with other schools in the state and region were held, and annual productions were presented to the public. As long as the concerts and productions were organized, Bob volunteered to draw the program covers.

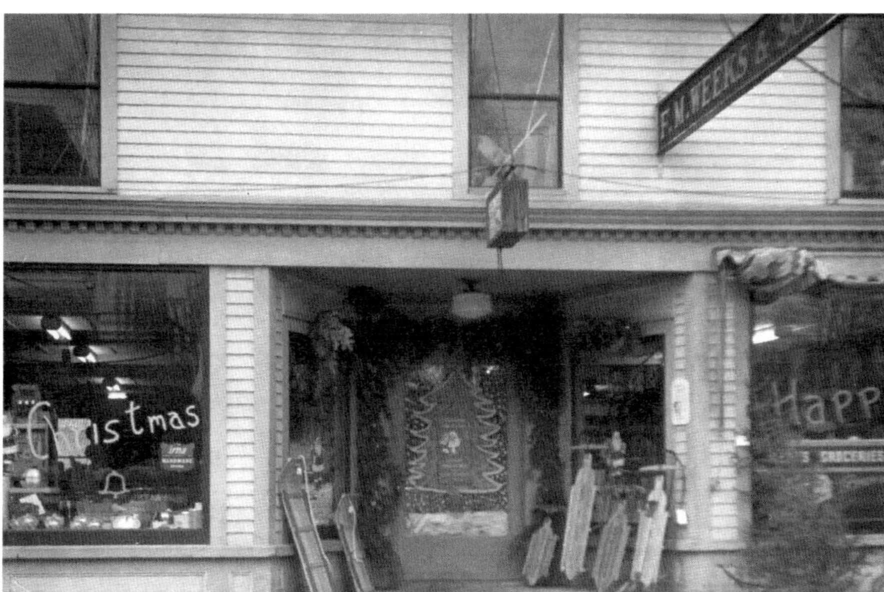

F.M. Weeks & Sons, established in 1880, was Meredith's oldest store. *Courtesy of Meredith Historical Society.*

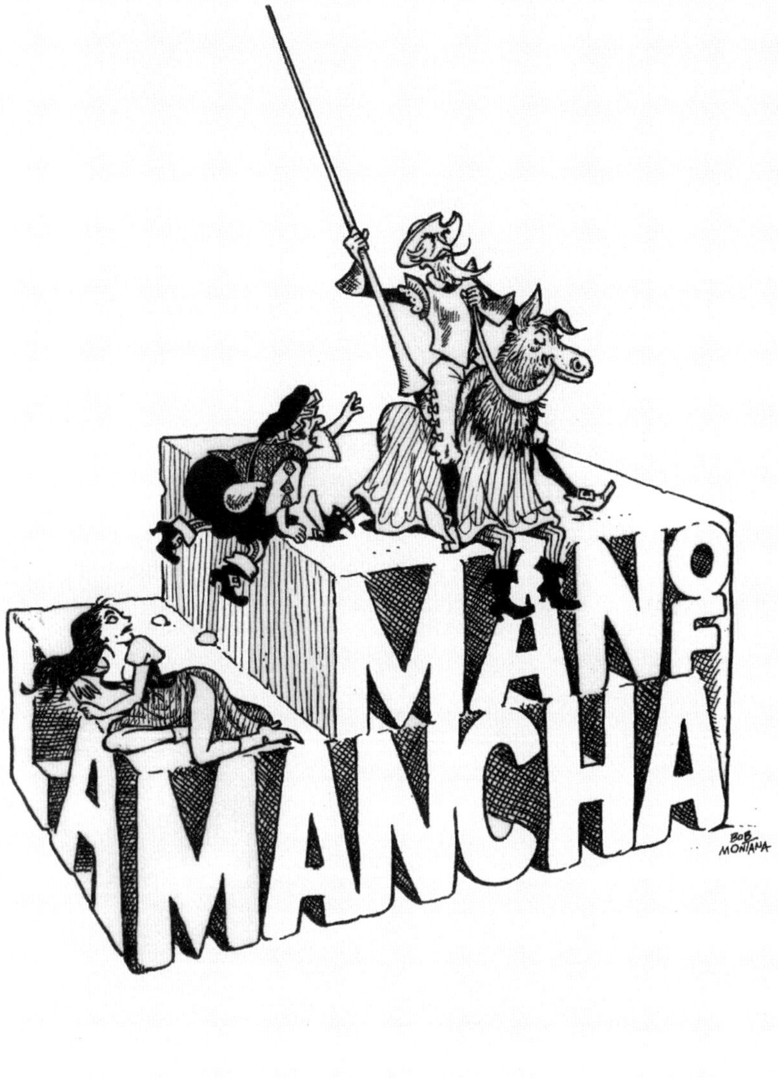

The program cover Bob created for the Inter-Lakes High School's production of *Man of La Mancha*. *Courtesy of Bruce Heald.*

Meredith was not the only town in the Lakes Region that underwent painful changes. Neighboring Laconia became a product of urban renewal and saw many of its historic buildings destroyed. In the early 1970s, Laconia's Belknap Mill, the country's oldest unaltered brick textile mill,

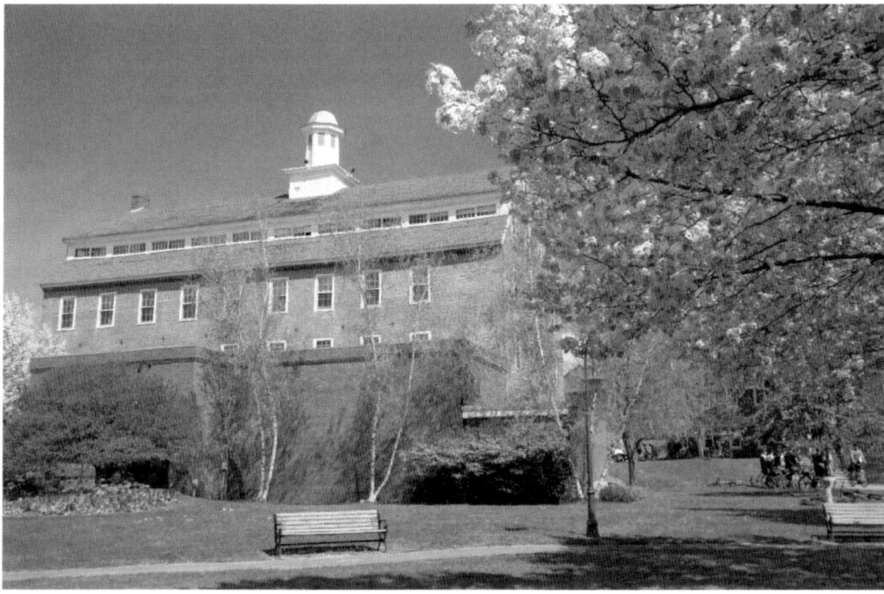

The historic Belknap Mill in Laconia was threatened with demolition during the 1970s and was featured in a Sunday *Archie*. *Photo by Harrison Haas.*

was faced with demolition. Built in 1823, it was one of several mills along the Winnipesaukee River that had turned the city into the hosiery capital of the world. In the late 1960s, due to changes in the workforce, the mill closed its doors. City officials and most residents wanted it removed from the landscape. A fierce, nationally publicized battle to save the structure was led by several local businessmen. Support for its preservation came from all across the country, especially from the towns surrounding Laconia. Bob offered his endorsement of the preservation effort by featuring the mill in a 1973 Sunday *Archie*.

The Lakes Region experienced a turbulent transition from the past into modern times. By the time Bob drew the Belknap Mill into the *Archie* strip, he was semi-retired. His dream and goal was to spend more time as a gentleman farmer on his organic farm in Meredith. In the early 1970s, many of the themes in the daily *Archie* strips saw the inclusion of subjects such as gardening, goats and beehives. In the spring of 1970, an article ran in the *Laconia Evening Citizen* that described Bob's passion for organic gardening:

> *However, what some of* [Montana's] *fans may not know is his love for animals and farming, and his devotion to it. This farmer raises goats,*

> *sheep, chickens and roosters and eventually will invest in quarter horses and heavy steers. His beautiful farm high on a hill top is a perfect setting. His green fields are rich and fertile with organic planting now in progress. Bob became very interested in this pure form of planting a couple of years ago and realized that unless the fields and pastures are returned back to the soil, we shall all become a society of well-fed sick people. His fields have not had any DDT or insecticides sprayed or spread on them in any way for the last 25 years, and only fertilizer is used. As Bob says, "I would rather find a worm in my apple than DDT in my stomach."*
>
> *There is a beautiful ten-foot-deep pond next to the barns in the back of the house well stocked with large-mouth bass where the family enjoys fishing in the spring; in the summer, it is used for swimming. Bob Montana is a very busy man, but never so busy that he cannot stop and chat. It's no wonder the people in Meredith are very proud of this celebrity—he's a pretty nice guy.*[80]

Today, organic farming is a highly accepted and desired method of producing food. When Bob became an organic farmer in the 1960s, the term automatically brought to mind visions of an environmental extremist. He was way ahead of his time, and he was a visionary. Yet because of the wholesome lifestyle he had chosen, he was often described as a non-conformist. He decided to tackle this label head-on in *Archie*. In one strip, it was Jughead's turn to be taunted, as he stood off by himself at the bus stop instead of standing with the rest of the gang. Unaffected by the names they called him—including "non-conformist"—he was the only one that remained dry when the bus splashed the entire group with mud during its arrival. Bob was sending a message to teenagers that perhaps those who think and do things differently often have the best ideas. He could have also been sending a rebuttal to those who had placed a label on him because of his lifestyle.

Several years had passed between the time of the zoning crisis in Meredith and Bob's semi-retirement. Meredith Bay had remained pristine and beautiful. It was Bob Montana, the non-conformist, and Chet Brickett who had paddled out in the dark of the night to hang the banner on that island. Had they not had the courage to do it, the outcome of the battle to save Meredith Bay might have been far different. Bob consistently remained true to himself—even if others placed labels on him. By doing so, he was one of the few that were able to quietly generate positive changes for the generations of today and tomorrow.

Chapter 17

A Lasting Legacy

Bob Montana showed me what integrity looked like. He showed me what quiet strength looked like. He showed me what proper priorities looked like and how important family and self-respect is.
—Steve Hulse, 2013

Cross-country skiing was a popular winter activity for the Montana family. The acreage surrounding the family home offered plenty of space for cross-country ski trails, a benefit that allowed Bob to exercise during the winter while remaining close to the drawing board. Downhill skiing was a thing of the past, as his contract allowed him to participate only in the more mundane sports in order to prevent him from injuring his arms or hands.

January 4, 1975, began as a day perfect for skiing and spending time outdoors. It would, however, end in unspeakable tragedy. Snowfall had been generous that winter, leaving no lack of skiers' white gold across the landscape. It was Saturday, and Paige, her future husband, David Kuether, Ray and Don were relaxing together with Bob on the farm.

The lure of the outdoors proved to be too much for the five of them, and they took off on cross-country skis, with the kids in the lead. The depth of the snow was deep, proving to be a challenge to maneuver through, and Bob had begun to lag behind. Ray gave a quick glance back and saw his father collapsed in the snow. In an instant, their world changed forever. David made desperate attempts to revive him, but Bob, like his father, died almost instantly of a massive heart attack. He was fifty-four years old.[81]

Lynn and her husband, Paul, were living in Massachusetts and rushed to Meredith as soon as they were notified. The family gathered once more at the farmhouse as they had so many times before, but this time was far different. Bob was gone forever, and his family tried to comprehend how they could go on without him. His death left a huge hole in each one of their lives.

The shock of Bob's sudden and untimely passing was felt deeply in Meredith, across the nation and throughout the world. Services were private, as Bob disliked funerals and did not want a public event at the time of his passing. In addition, it was estimated that approximately four thousand mourners might attend his memorial service. Quickly finding an appropriate location for such a large number of people in the middle of a very snowy New Hampshire winter would have been virtually impossible.

The staff of the *Laconia Evening Citizen* immediately reported on the death of their dear friend and offered readers insight as to what kind of man Bob Montana had been:

> *News of the death of Bob Montana, creator of the* Archie *comic strip, carried daily in newspapers in this and foreign countries, brings to hundreds the feeling they have lost a friend, a person greatly respected. Some years ago, a magazine ran an article titled "Has Success Spoiled Rock Hudson?" Other magazines followed with articles, applying the test to other celebrities. Bob Montana was not included. From the time he was a student at Manchester High School, down through the years he has made his home in Meredith, there have never been any questions about changes in his personality. He remained to the end the same approachable individual, eager to be of help, sincerely interested in the well-being of others.*
>
> *Our last conversation provided a typical example of his desire to assist fellow humans. We were asked by a Concord man if we could arrange a meeting with Montana for him and a teenage nephew, winner of prizes in drawing contests, who might benefit from suggestions as to the methods he should pursue to become a professional artist.*
>
> *"I shall be most happy to see this young man. I think it is important to extend a helping hand. I know in my own case I received suggestions when starting out that helped me immensely. I feel obligated to assist in the same manner and will give your friend and the boy all the time they want."*
>
> *Success did not spoil Bob Montana.*[82]

The Montana family spent the spring and early summer attempting to rebuild their lives. However, death and sadness once again found a way into their lives. At the time of Bob's death, Roberta had already been diagnosed with cancer. Having to face life without her beloved son stole her will to live, and she died in July. Again, the Montana family grieved, as did her friends in Meredith.

Two of the town's most cherished residents had passed away within months of each other. Meredith came together in August for what they called Bob Montana Night. The event was sponsored by the Meredith American Revolution Bicentennial Committee, held at the Inter-Lakes Elementary School and organized by longtime friends Bob Valliere and Ray Roux. The Montana family assisted by providing some of Bob's original drawings, sketches and artwork, along with the movies he had directed and produced. The event gave the people of Meredith an opportunity to reflect on Bob's extraordinary life and remember all that he had given to his hometown, the Lakes Region and beyond.[83] His life was celebrated, but those in attendance knew what a great man the world had lost. Life in Meredith without Bob Montana would never be the same.

The next Meredith Town Report was dedicated to the late Bob Montana and included his photo with the following caption:

> *Creator of the internationally famous comic strip* Archie, *Bob always found time to contribute his talents as cartoonist, artist, actor and musician to assist community projects. Many of the scenes and characters of* Archie *were based on local events, places and people. During his extensive travels throughout the country and the world, he was an unofficial ambassador of Meredith, spreading the word of beauty and attractions of this area.*

What the town report could not include were the memories of Bob that family and friends held dear in their hearts. Every person who had been blessed to have known him was also fortunate enough to have been left with a piece of Bob's wisdom that he had thoughtfully and carefully customized for each one of them. In some cases, the course of their life was changed by his words.

Marie Jose Malarge, the young French au pair who had stayed with the Montanas, is today a wife and the mother of two adult daughters. She described the day she heard of Bob's death as well as the appreciation she has for all that Bob and Peg taught her:

> *It was a letter from Lynn that informed me of Bob's death. The ground disappeared from under me, and it took me a long time to realize how much he*

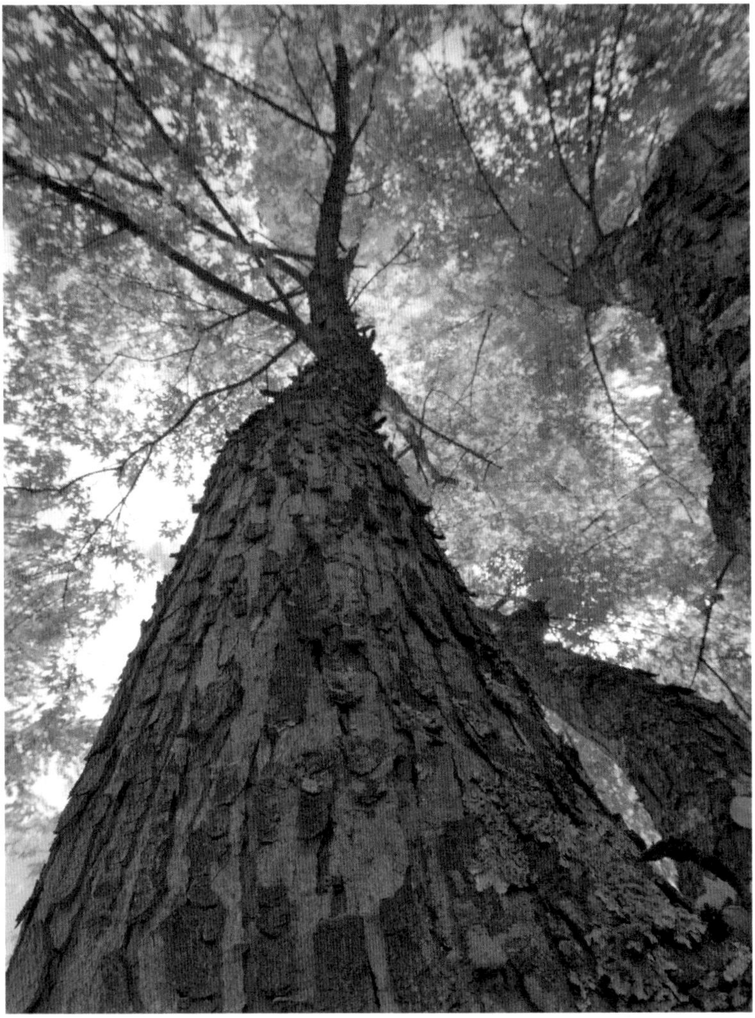

An oak tree on the shore of Meredith Bay reaches for the stars, something Bob encouraged all to do. *Photo by Harrison Haas.*

would be missed by everyone around him. I thought of everyone, particularly each member of the family and friends, trying to imagine how they would live without him. Peggy was a strong person, and I knew she'd continue as before (almost, only because Bob wasn't there anymore as a guide).

He was such a profoundly thinking person who gently decided how to live and maintain a harmonious life on the farm—for everyone and for me, then living in France. Between art and nature, I try to live every day like he showed me.

As for Bob and Peggy's lessons, everything I do here is what they transmitted to me. I have passed along the same to my daughters, who are now twenty-five and twenty-three years old. I've noticed, now that they have passed out of adolescence, that they have taken examples of what I learned when I lived with the Montana family.[84]

Bruce Heald gained wisdom from his friendship and conversations with Bob, eventually earning his doctorate and becoming the author of nearly fifty books. He was distraught when he learned of Bob's death, but Bruce has lived by the sage advice that was given to him by his friend:

That day when he went out cross-country skiing…when I learned that he had died, I was completely devastated; he was far too young.

What Bob gave to me and what I carry with me today is the idea that I should always reach out and expand my horizons. When I first arrived in Meredith, I was a musician, and all I concentrated on was music. Bob urged me to look further than that—to try something different. I did that back then, and I still do that today.

Bob was my buddy. He was a Norman Rockwell. He was the most talented, humorous, light-hearted man I have ever met, and he loved the town of Meredith. He was a great family man, and it was his family that meant more to him than anything else.[85]

Steve Hulse gained a new outlook from Bob on how to deal with the discomfort he felt when being acknowledged for his talents. The advice could not have been better coming from a man who grew up on the stage during one of America's greatest decades of entertainment. Steve explained the conversation he had with Bob while they were together in Boston:

The summer of 1970, Bob, Peg and several of the kids came down to Boston for the weekend. I had arranged the brass and strings for a debut album (vinyl back then) for a singer named Jimmy Helms. The album had been released, and he was doing a weeklong gig in a Boston club called Paul's Mall. When I found out Bob and his family would be in town, I invited them to attend Jimmy's gig, which had a full contingent of horns, playing arrangements I'd written for the album.

We got a good table and enjoyed a set, and at the end, Jimmy introduced me to the audience as the arranger of his new album and of the arrangements the horns had just played. I stood up only partway to the applause, weakly

> *waved my hand and immediately sat back down, surprised and humbled by the unexpected introduction and applause.*
>
> *Before we even left the club, Bob pulled me aside and said, "Schultz, you've got to learn to take your introductions and praise with pride and confidence. You need to stand up straight, smile and be the person they're applauding. That's no time for humility, whether it's real or not. Stand up like a man and thank them as if you owned the place and they were your guests." His voice never rose, but his intent was focused and serious, the most serious I ever saw him. He slapped me on the back, and we left the club. Had I not been as young as I was, I no doubt would have learned much more from him. As it was, he remains a man of immense creativity, humor, wisdom and integrity, in my mind and in my heart.*[86]

In September 1994, *NH Crossroads*, a television program that spotlighted New Hampshire people and places, ran a segment on Bob Montana and his connection to Meredith. Peg, Lynn, Ray and Don were there for the taping, as were several of Bob's friends who still lived in town. Ray spoke of his father and his relationship with the *Archie* comic strip, saying, "He was Archie. You don't create this person every day without becoming him." As Ray continued, he explained his father's philosophy of life: "He was about gathering experiences, not so much things."

Lynn described their adventures while they lived in foreign countries but said that life back home in Meredith was just as exciting. "There was always something going on," she said. "As soon as he finished one project, he'd start on another one. He had a knack for turning an ordinary event into one of an atmosphere of pleasure and beauty." She concluded by saying, "He was a great dad."

Bob's friends Bob Bennett, Ray Huckins, Dick Guion and Bob Valliere gathered around a table at Chase's, a local restaurant, each telling stories about the man who had been such a great friend to them. Ray Huckins, Meredith's postmaster who appeared as one in the strip, felt it was always a treat when Bob came into the post office. "He was always the same…always had a joke," he said. Dick Guion added, "Bob was everyone's friend, and he certainly kept things jumping." Bob Valliere thoroughly enjoyed his friendship with Meredith's most famous resident, laughing about how Bob always drew him into the comic strip with a cigar even though he didn't smoke them. He hesitated for a moment and then said that Bob was still sorely missed.

It was Bob Bennett who had so much to say about Bob Montana, both during that episode of *NH Crossroads* as well as in his newspaper column a year earlier. He shared his thoughts about Meredith's beloved cartoonist and celebrity:

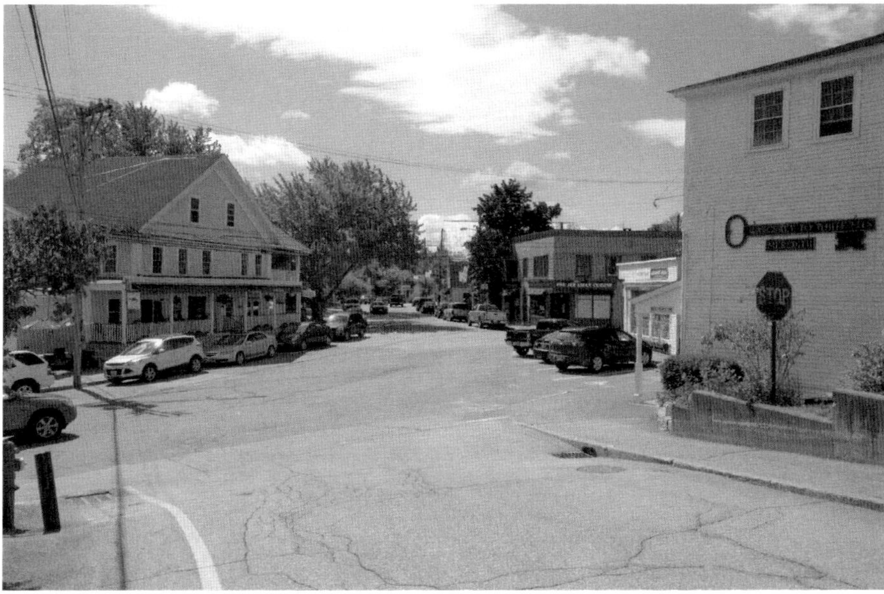

A contemporary view of Main Street in Bob's beloved hometown of Meredith. *Photo by Harrison Haas.*

> *The one person I can truly call a friend would be the late Bob Montana. He probably has done more to put Meredith "on the map" than anyone else I can think of.*
>
> *When Bob and Peg were married in 1946, they came to Meredith and spent the summer at the Cowing cottage over on Lake Waukewan. After Labor Day, they moved into town and set up housekeeping in the Abby Cowing home on Lang Street, at the junction of Lang and South Main Street, next to Dr. Turley's home. When they moved in that fall, I was a neighbor. I could look cross lot and down to see Bob working on his "Archie" comic strip at his drawing board in the back room. He spent many hours at that table.*
>
> *On many occasions, I would be going to bed around midnight, look out and see Bob with his head on his hand trying to come up with an idea that could be used in his comic strip. Come early morning, when I was getting ready to go to work, Bob would still be at the drawing board, as he probably spent the night.*
>
> *Bob did so many things to entertain others, and he was tireless in these ventures.*[87]

Shortly after the episode of *NH Crossroads* aired, Meredith's schoolchildren headed back to the classroom. Inter-Lakes High School art teacher Sharon

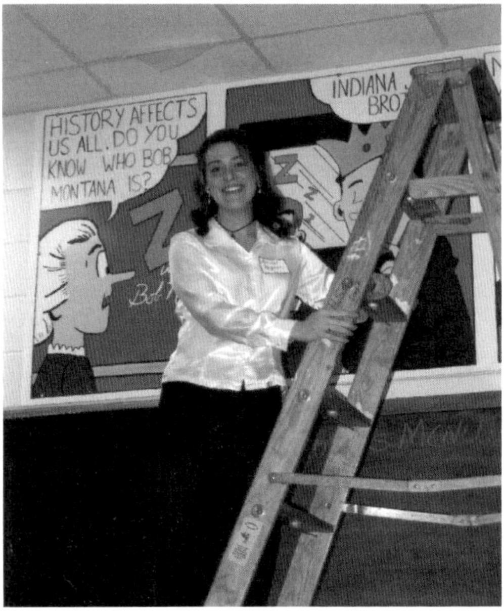

Kristal Keysar poses in 1996 with the mural she created honoring cartoonist Bob Montana. © *Montana family*.

LaFond gave independent art student Kristal Keysar an assignment. Kristal was asked to create a dedication to Bob Montana as an effort directed at teaching students about the world-famous cartoonist who had lived and worked in their hometown. The young art student took her assignment seriously, designing and painting a four-foot by thirty-two-foot mural that posed the question, "Who Is Bob Montana?" Using an *Archie* comic book for reference, she worked feverishly in her spare time after school. Kristal did not rest until she knew the mural and the accompanying plaque would be finished for the fiftieth anniversary of the publication of the first *Archie* comic strip in February 1996.

A crowd gathered for the official dedication ceremony that included family members, local residents, friends and Bob's ever-faithful assistants, Ruth Harding, Jeff Cuddy and Raleigh Wilkerson. Raleigh had first worked with Bob while teaching at the Village Gallery and was part of the group that stayed to reminisce after the event. The mural remains on permanent display in the Inter-Lakes cafeteria and continues to be a creative reminder of Bob Montana.[88]

In 1999, author John Clayton published a book entitled *New Hampshire: The Way I See It*, which includes a chapter dedicated to Bob Montana. In it, former assistant Jeff Cuddy described the great cartoonist as a kind and generous man and then described the talent he saw in Bob:

> *He would send me the strips in the mail, rolled up inside nylon stocking tubes...it was really a great privilege to work with him because he taught me everything I know about comics. When I was learning his technique, I would stand at his shoulder and watch him, and he was just so deft. He could just make those characters come alive.*

After Bob passed away, Jeff tried to continue the strip but quickly realized his abilities fell far short of what was required in order for him to carry on with it. He stated it simply: "Bob was a genius; I couldn't keep up."

Bill Allen, son of barber Jesse Allen, grew up in Meredith and described how exciting it was to be a child in the town that Bob Montana called home:

> *Bob Montana was the man who put Meredith on the map. To the children of Meredith, he was a celebrity.* Archie *was a top comic when we were growing up, and to us, he was a landmark figure. Bob was a friend to all, and everyone had the highest respect for him. He was way ahead of his time in so many ways. The things he did for Meredith he did for no reason other than they were the right things to do, and not with any expectations of making money, as some people do.*
>
> *I spent twenty-four years in the army, and of course, no matter where I was, I would always say that I was from Meredith, the home of Bob Montana. Everyone knew who Bob was. He made me proud of Meredith even though the town had its challenges. What Bob did for me was nurture a desire in me to come home, to always return to Meredith.*[89]

Bob's children—his "awards," as he called them—carry out his legacy each and every day. Paige is a retired Meredith schoolteacher. Ray works within

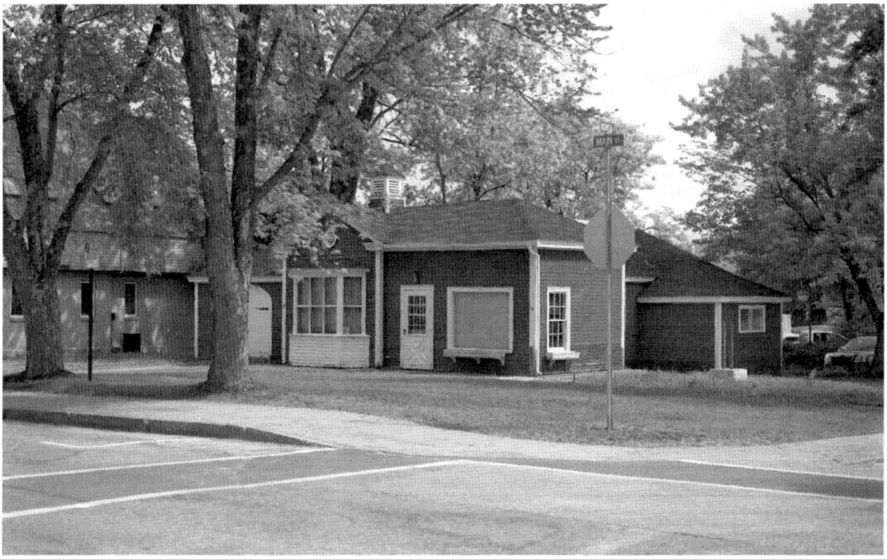

Today, the former Village Gallery is dwarfed by the trees Bob planted in 1967. *Photo by Harrison Haas.*

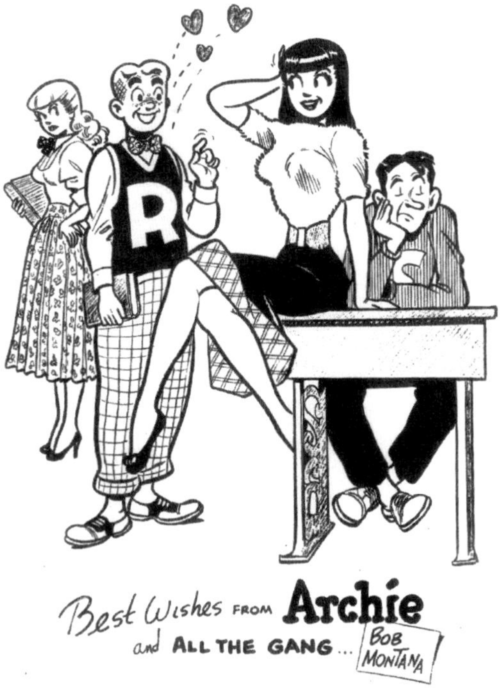

© *Montana family.*

the solar energy industry and is also a professional musician. Don works as a carpenter and is a drummer for the CD Woodbury Band, the number-one roots/blues band in the state of Washington. The band's music is played throughout the world. Lynn is the owner of Montana Framing and is a designer/framer for a Meredith frame shop. She possesses an eye for design and color that could be matched only by her father. Through the years, they have all continued to give back to the communities in which they live and work. Bob and Peg were loving and dedicated parents, and they taught their children well.

In 2010, Bob received a long-overdue honor. He was inducted into the Eisner Hall of Fame, one of the highest honors that can be bestowed upon a cartoonist.[90] Nearly forty years after his death, his genius, creativity and the impact of his life's work still shine brightly. Archie, the iconic and loveable teenager that bubbled up from the center of Bob's creative mind, lives on and has become an epic part of American history.

This remarkably gifted and humble man did not force his talents upon anyone; rather, he traveled through life in his own quiet way and with goodness in his heart. The words of Mahatma Gandhi beautifully encapsulate the extraordinary life of Bob Montana: "In a gentle way, you can shake the world."

Notes

Chapter 1

1. Montana the Cowboy Banjoist, "My Greatest Venture," *Metronome*, 1926.
2. Ibid.

Chapter 2

3. Hengen, "Meredith's Historic Architecture."
4. Bob Montana, "Bob Montana."
5. Fay King, a female cartoonist during the 1920s, has been described as one of the greatest cartoonists of the time.

Chapter 4

6. Rube Goldberg was an engineer, Pulitzer Prize–winning cartoonist, author, sculptor and inventor. He was one of the founders of the National Cartoonist Society.
7. Bob Montana, "Bob Montana."
8. Cord Elliot, "Meet Bob Montana," MLJ publication, date unknown.
9. Peg Montana, "Bob Montana the Man."
10. McClure Newspaper Syndicate, press release, date unknown.

Chapter 5

11. *Meredith News*, "Cartoonist Plans to Make Meredith His Home," July 18, 1946.
12. Peg Montana, "Bob Montana the Man."
13. *Meredith News,* "Archie Wins Bout Aided by Dr. Turley," January 20, 1950.
14. Unknown newspaper, "Comic Strip Town," October 13, 1963.
15. *Meredith News*, "Bob Montana, Cartoonist, Entertains P.T.A.," October 21, 1948.
16. *Meredith News*, "I Wanna Be Borned in Meredith, Says Real Life Veronica, Paige Montana," February 3, 1949.
17. Ken Gould, "Creating Smiling Archie and His Gang is Hard Work Says Meredith Artist Bob Montana, Who Labors 60 Hours a Week," *Meredith News*, October 6, 1949.
18. *Meredith News*, "Montana Buys Farm to Live Here for Good," July 13, 1950.

Chapter 6

19. Lake Winnipesaukee Museum, "Boating in the Lakes Region," www.lwhs.us/boatingwhereto1949.htm.
20. *Meredith News,* "Letter to the Editor," March 12, 1953.
21. Unknown newspaper clipping, date unknown.

Chapter 7

22. Bob Montana, "Bob Montana."
23. *Meredith News*, "Bob Montana Wins Playwright Prize," April 17, 1952.
24. *Meredith News*, unknown article, June 26, 1952.
25. *Meredith News,* "Players Annual Show Opens Thursday," June 3, 1954.

Chapter 8

26. *Meredith News*, "Meredith People Figure in R.R. Holdup," January 26, 1927.
27. *Meredith News*, "Village Players See Film Made on Tryouts for Movie," March 15, 1956.

Chapter 9

28. *Meredith News*, "Boy, Girl…Girl, Boy?? Bob Montana Was Prepared," July 28, 1955.
29. *Meredith News*, "Archie and Bob Move to King Features with Much Fanfare," December 8, 1955.
30. Bob Montana, "From Archie to Archery," *Archery*, April 1956.

Chapter 10

31. *Meredith News*, letter from Roberta Montana, January 29, 1959.
32. *Meredith News*, "Centennial Celebration is Overwhelming Success," August 20, 1959.
33. Ibid.
34. Bob Montana, "Studio Visit," unknown publication, March 1961.
35. The Sandwich Fair, "A Bit of History," http://www.thesandwichfair.com/html/fair_origins.html.
36. *Meredith News*, "In and About Meredith," October 10, 1961.
37. *Meredith News*, "Village Players to Shine Again Saturday Evening," March 28, 1963.
38. Robert D. Bennett, "I Remember When," *Meredith News*, December 29, 1993.

Chapter 11

39. *Meredith News,* "In and About Meredith," August 13, 1964.
40. *Meredith News*, "Montana Goes to England," September 3, 1964.
41. *Meredith News*, "In and About Meredith," January 21, 1965.
42. Werner Bamberger, "Storm-Battered Michelangelo is Due Here Today," *New York Times*, date unknown.
43. *Meredith News*, "Bob Montana Describes Harrowing Atlantic Crossing," April 21, 1966.
44. Lynn Montana, interview with author, January 2013.
45. Marie Jose Malarge, e-mail to author, December 2012.
46. Dave Karlen's Original Art Blog, "National Cartoonist Society Profile: Bob Montana," http://www.davekarlenoriginalartblogspot.com/2010/09/national-cartoonist-society-profile-bob.html.

CHAPTER 12

47. *Cartoonist PROfiles*, date unknown.
48. *Meredith News*, "In and About Meredith," November 22, 1956.
49. *Meredith News*, "Wandering Pig Finds Home at Corliss Farm," October 13, 1960.
50. Bob Bolduc, interviews with author, September 2012 and May 2013.
51. The Funspot, "Funspot 50th Anniversary History," http://funspotnh.com/history.htm.
52. *Meredith News*, "First and Last Customer at Bob's Texaco," August 4, 1966.

CHAPTER 13

53. *Cartoonist PROfiles*, date unknown.
54. *Meredith News*, "Main Street Has New Look," February 2, 1967.
55. *Cartoonist PROfiles*, date unknown.
56. Paul Miller, e-mail to author, February 2013.
57. Steve Hulse, e-mail to author, December 2012.
58. Ibid.

CHAPTER 14

59. NH.Searchroots.com, "History of Meredith, Belknap County, New Hampshire," http://www.nh.searchroots.com/documents/History_Meredith_NH.txt.
60. *Meredith News*, "Time Capsules Buried in Meredith," July 10, 1969. DVD copies of *Meredith: The First 200 Years* and *The Close Shave* are available for purchase through the Meredith Public Library.
61. *Meredith News*, "Tow of Meredith Honored as a Bicentennial Community," December 28, 1974.

CHAPTER 15

62. United States Organizations (USO) is a congressionally chartered nonprofit organization that lifts the spirits of America's troops and their families.
63. *Meredith News*, "Archie Creator and Jazz Stick Off to Europe," October 2, 1952.
64. *Meredith News*, "Montana Returns After Entertaining G.I.'s in Europe," November 20, 1952
65. Bob Montana, letter to Elmer Messner, February 6, 1960.
66. Al Kramer, "Artists Tour U.S. Hospitals in Asia," unknown newspaper, 1968.

67. Ibid.
68. *Meredith News*, "Bob Montana Named '69 N.H. Easter Seal Co-Chairman," March 6, 1969.
69. *Meredith News*, "Bill Veeck to be Feature Speaker at Easter Seal Banquet," March 13, 1969.
70. *Meredith News*, "Archie and Bob Lead Record Breaking Drive," July 3, 1969.
71. *Meredith News*, "Co-Chairman Easter Seal Drive," March 19, 1970.

Chapter 16

72. Steve Hulse, e-mail to author, December 2012.
73. *Cartoonist PROfiles*, date unknown.
74. Ibid.
75. June Tyhurst, "Comic Characters Almost Like Real," *Daily O'Collegian*, September 25, 1969.
76. *Meredith News*, "New Habitat Condominium Towers," August 22, 1968.
77. *Meredith News*, "Two Important Meetings for Meredith Residents," October 3, 1968.
78. *Meredith News*, "Meredith Reaffirms Vote on Height of Buildings," April 17, 1969.
79. *Meredith News*, "Sixtieth Wedding Anniversary," January 25, 1973.
80. Aline Jacobs, "Bob Montana Reveals Interest in Farming and Animals," *Laconia Evening Citizen*, May 23, 1970.

Chapter 17

81. Lynn Montana, e-mail to author, February 2013.
82. *Laconia Evening Citizen*, "Success Did Not Spoil Bob Montana," January 6, 1975.
83. *Meredith News*, "The Close Shave to Highlight Bob Montana Night," August 14, 1975.
84. Marie Jose Malarge, e-mail to author, December 2012.
85. Bruce Heald, interview with author, March 2013.
86. Steve Hulse, e-mail to author, December 2012.
87. Robert D. Bennett, "I Remember When," *Meredith News*, December 22, 1993.
88. James A. Kimble, "An Artist Remembered," *Meredith News*, February 28, 1996.
89. Bill Allen, interview with author, May 2013.
90. The Eisner Hall of Fame annually inducts some of the best artists and writers of comic books and strips.

Bibliography

Brandt, Del. "The Man Who Made Us Laugh." *Weirs Times*, December 31, 1998, 5–46.

Clayton, John. *New Hampshire: The Way I See It*. Portsmouth, NH: Peter E. Randall, 1999.

Heald, Bruce, Ph.D. *Meredith: Then and Now*. Charleston, SC: Arcadia, 2005.

Hengen, Elizabeth Durfee. "Meredith's Historic Architecture: A Reference Guide." Unpublished paper, December 2000.

Montana, Bob. *Archie: The Complete Daily Newspaper Comics, 1946–1948*. San Diego, CA: IDW Publishing, 2010.

———. *Archie's Sunday Finest*. San Diego, CA: IDW Publishing, 2012.

———. "Bob Montana." Unpublished paper, date unknown.

Montana, Peg. "Bob Montana the Man." Unpublished paper, date unknown.

Additional Resources

"Archie Comics." *NH Crossroads*, Episode 1344, DVD. Durham, NH: New Hampshire Public Television, September 1994.

Belknap Mill Society. Bob Montana collection.

Bob Montana Diary, 1937–38. Courtesy of the Montana family.

Bob Montana original *Archie* comic strips, 1946–75. Courtesy of the Montana family.

Bob Montana scrapbooks and home movies, 1927–75. Courtesy of the Montana family.
Jesse Allen photographs. Courtesy of the Allen family.
Laconia Evening Citizen
Meredith Historical Society. Photographs, programs and artwork collections.
Meredith News
Meredith Town Reports, 1962, 1963, 1974 and 1975.
Montana, Bob. *The Close Shave*. Film directed by John Jewett and Bob Montana. Meredith, NH: Meredith Village Players, 1952.
———. *Meredith: The First 200 Years*. Film directed by Bob Montana. Meredith, NH, 1968.

WEBSITES

Dave Karlen's Original Art Blog. "National Cartoonist Society Profile: Bob Montana." http://www.davekarlenoriginalartblogspot.com/2010/09/national-cartoonist-society-profile-bob.html.
The Funspot. "Funspot 50th Anniversary History." http://funspotnh.com/history.htm.
NH.Searchroots.com. "History of Meredith, Belknap County, New Hampshire." http://www.nh.searchroots.com/documents/History_Meredith_NH.txt.
The Sandwich Fair. "A Bit of History." http://www.thesandwichfair.com/html/fair_origins.html
Toucan Blog. "Will Eisner Hall of Fame." http://www.comic-con.org/toucan/will-eisner-hall-of-fame-now-on-line.

INTERVIEWS

Allen, William and Lynn. Interviews with author, January and May 2013.
Bolduc, Robert. Interviews with author, September 2012 and May 2013.
Heald, Bruce, Ph.D. Interview with author, March 2013.
Karagianas, Peter. Interview with author, January 2013.
Lawton, Robert. Interview with author, December 2012.
Miller, Paul. Interview with author, February 2013.
Montana, Lynn. Interviews with author, 2011–13.

About the Author

For almost a decade, historian Carol Lee Anderson has written articles detailing local histories for newspapers throughout the Lakes Region of central New Hampshire. She has served as a board member for a number of historical societies, and in 2009, she became a founder and first president of the award-winning Gunstock Mountain Historical Society in Gilford. Her first book, *The History of Gunstock: Skiing in the Belknap Mountains*, was published by The History Press in 2011. Shortly after being released, it received the prestigious Skade Award from the International Skiing History Association.

Carol lives in the Lakes Region with her husband, son and daughter. For more information about her works, visit CarolLeeAnderson.com.